8/95

BECOMING

☆ ☆ ☆

AMERICAN

BECOMING

☆ ☆ ☆

AMERICAN

Young People in the
American Revolution

P. M. Zall

LINNET BOOKS

1993

The paper used in this publication meets the minimum requirements
of American National Standard for Information Sciences
—Permanence of Paper for Printed Library Materials,
ANSI Z39.48—1984. ♾

Library of Congress Cataloging-in-Publication Data

Zall, Paul M.
Becoming American : young people in the
American revolution / by P. M. Zall.
p.   cm.
Summary: Includes letters, diaries, and journals of
over twenty young people from all walks of life,
reflecting their experiences in the pivotal period
in American history 1767 to 1789.
1. United States—History—Revolution, 1775–1783
—Personal narratives—Juvenile literature.
2. United States—History—Revolution, 1775–1783
—Participation, Juvenile—Juvenile literature.
3. United States—History—Revolution, 1775–1783
—Children—Juvenile literature.
4. Children—United States—History
—18th century—Juvenile literature.
5. Youth—United States—History
—18th century—Juvenile literature.
[1. United States—History—Revolution, 1775–1783
—Personal narratives.
2. United States—History —Confederation, 1783–1789
—Personal narratives.
3. Youths' writings.]   I. Title
E275.Z34   1993   92-40199   973.3'8—dc20
ISBN 0-208-02355-0 (alk. paper)

Printed in the United States of America

For Brian J. Zall

CONTENTS

PREFACE

This book is divided into six sections, roughly paralleling the progress of the American Revolution through to the inauguration of Washington as first president. It contains excerpts from writings by twenty-three young people, all under the age of twenty-one, who documented the events of their lives in journals, diaries, letters, and the like.

Each section is introduced generally to orient the reader to the matters ahead; each excerpt is introduced by a note which places the writer's words in their immediate social context. The words themselves are unchanged. Any doubt about their meaning is explained in brackets immediately following them. Some abridgment has been made of the texts, and spelling, punctuation, and paragraphing have been modernized. Occasionally old capitalization has been retained to contribute to the flavor of the episodes.

Wherever possible each excerpt has been drawn from original sources, either in the writers' own handwriting or from an early, credible printed source in a rare book or periodical. Almost all these manuscripts and rare books are in the Huntington Library, San Marino, California, and are reprinted through permission of the curators. So are the contemporary illustrations. Special thanks is due to Curator of Manuscripts, Mary Robertson, for permission to reprint excerpts of Baylor Hill's text, and the Archivist John P. Riley of the Mount Vernon Ladies' Association Library, for his assistance and permission to reprint excerpts of Bob Lewis's text. Sources of the documents are given at the end of each excerpt, and biographical notes on the later life of each writer are included in an Afterword.

Rather than include a bibliography, I recommend as most appropriate for these diaries a short book, *The Birth of the Republic, 1763–89* by Edmund S. Morgan. The revised edition of 1977 is available in paperback from The University of Chicago Press.

For help in each stage of research and editing, I have to thank Jennifer Lee Martinez, Marty Ridge, Debby Roberts, Bob Gunderson, Leona Schonfeld, Pat Smith, and the many teenaged consultants and library staff who volunteered time and patience. Diantha Thorpe worked hardest of all.

P. M. Z.
San Marino, California
Winter 1993

INTRODUCTION:
BECOMING AMERICAN

When people heard about the research for this book, the first question they asked was, "How did kids differ in those days?" Their curiosity was about the young people themselves—what they thought, how they lived, what they liked or didn't like to do. And it is no wonder. Although much has been written by adults about the American Revolution for teenagers to read, not much written *by* teenagers of that time is available.

How did they differ? They were older. If they survived birth, they had to grow up in a hurry or never get to grow up at all. Not just war, disease, hunger, and the rest of the ills that beset developing countries, but stress and similar emotional wounds bruised young people then as now. But "being older" meant being drawn into society as an active participant, a necessary and valuable asset to the vigorous life of a new nation. It did not mean the useless premature aging seen in some societies today, where life experience is out of proportion to a young person's ability to deal constructively—or deal at all—with it.

My intent in doing this book was to let these young people speak directly to their peers of today, to show how they share the condition of humanity in times of strain, and how they did not merely endure, but survived and even thrived. They became accustomed to upheaval, relocation, and uncertainty, accepting them as a way of life. They had a fresh view of events otherwise familiar to us in history and fiction, and although some did not live beyond the Revolutionary years, their words survive to show us what they were thinking and feeling as the new nation took shape.

This is why it is so important to hear their voices rather than some modern editor's version of what they should have said but probably did not. Not all could write—slaves, for instance—or Native Americans, whose own culture relied on word-of-mouth transmission in their own languages. But for Slave Andrew, whose testimony is from the official transcript of the Boston Massacre trial, and Charles Bourgatte, an apprentice whose testimony at the same trial was in French, the so-called "underclasses" of society are not represented here except in gossip. Neither, however, are representatives of the very rich, many of whom wrote in German, French, or Spanish, and whose diaries and letters present problems of translation.

Excerpts such as Slave Andrew's and Charles Bourgatte's were also selected to give readers the chance to compare one account with another and, when pertinent, to compare them with contemporary experience. This is true of others, as well. Solomon Drowne's visit to Newport contrasts with the wartime travels of Betsy Ambler; Jemima Condict's feelings about her family compare with Robert Morton's feelings about his own; Sam Webb's reaction to the blood and guts of war contrasts with Baylor Hill's; Charles Herbert's triumph over isolation in prison, where he hid his diary under floorboards and made his own pencils, compares with Nabby Adams's isolation in an alien land.

Some parallels with our contemporary failings are shocking. Robert Morton's experience of seeing his stepfather exiled as a *potential* subversive has its corollary among thousands of

Japanese-American young people whose families were interned at the time of World War II. Eben Denny's hostile reception by the Virginians he was fighting to defend has a familiar echo in the experience of Viet Nam. The mob violence suffered by Anne Rawle will be all too familiar to residents of today's inner cities.

The actual events of history are retold here only in summary, as backdrop to each excerpt. More important is to see such surprising phenomena as the independence displayed by girls in what we might think was a restrictive, male-dominated world. Jemima Condict of New Jersey, like Nancy Shippen of Pennsylvania and Rebecca Franks of New York, decided for herself when and who to marry, and *if* to marry, and commented with relish on the opposite sex. It may also surprise some to see the responsibility borne by such young persons, some of whom took care of family business for absent parents, or even national business with their parents. Some rose rapidly as military commanders or government officials. But we forget: there weren't many people on American soil 200 years ago, and the population was young by today's standards. Half the people in the country were under the age of sixteen, and the Declaration of Independence itself was composed by a thirty-two year-old, Thomas Jefferson.

The sense of time and space that pervades these excerpts is also arresting. Travel was difficult, tedious, and time-consuming, yet everyone traveled a lot and surprisingly, news traveled quickly. Jemima Condict in New Jersey had heard of the skirmishes at Lexington and Concord the day after they happened; Elijah Backus at Yale was getting near-daily bulletins (many of them inaccurate) on the progress of the war right up to the Battle of Saratoga. Armies traveled back and forth around Philadelphia so much that weary residents were often not sure which was coming and which was going. And on top of it, all the people seemed to know one another, or were related. Family ties were close and warm; the country was smaller; the literate population smaller still; and as the Revolution wore on, wartime marriages brought families from different regions together in networks of land, money, and political power.

The overall impression of these first-person accounts is of human resilience in times of upheaval. None of the writers celebrate the Revolution in the patriotic terms of today. Instead of pondering abstractions, they wonder about what would happen next. Their ambivalence to newfound freedom seems very much like that facing Soviet-bloc countries with the dissolution of the USSR in the early 1990s. Textbook theories of the "Rights of Man" or "Freedom, Equality, Fraternity" meant little, for instance, to young Bob Lewis shouldering the responsibility of squiring his aunt, Martha Washington, to the capital of New York, or to Martha Jefferson a few years earlier, trying to learn French in a hurry in a Paris convent.

When independence arrived it brought new options, new necessities, and shadowings of what was to come. John Quincy Adams was much more aware of the political significance of Shay's Rebellion than an earlier collegian, Elijah Backus, had been of the war. There *was* no enemy to oppose—only the much more frightening task of a government to construct. By the 1790s, with the war long over and Washington installed as president, people could take a good look at the nation they had fought for. Slaves, who once relied on word-of-mouth for political information, now had access to newspapers and also sermons published by their own preachers practicing as freedmen in the North. Along with abolitionists and other humanitarians, even they had the chance to meditate on and react to the paradox of slavery in a land dedicated to the proposition that all men were created equal. Likewise, concerned patriots anxious for a democratic republic to work would worry about the obvious fact that those wealthy and powerful before the war remained wealthy and powerful afterwards. But at least now the opportunity was within reach for them to take control of their lives, and to lead a better life than their parents had. This remains the essence of the American Dream.

The problems of a free people—race, religion, economic self-determination, social and cultural priorities—are alive and worth working out for each young person who wants to understand what it means to be an American. Although the writers of these accounts speak across 200 years, they handled similar problems for their times. Faced with change, some relished the chance to take on something new, while others withdrew into a private world of their own and still others ignored everything else but their own instant gratification. Theirs was an opportunity to grow up with their new country, and most took it. They learned to compromise, to stop being Virginians, or Bostonians, or Georgians, or Carolinians first, and foremost. They learned to be more. It took them some time, but they learned to become Americans.

Part I

☆ ☆ ☆

*From the Stamp Act
to the
Boston Tea Party*

1765–1775

Ten years before the Declaration of Independence nobody would have thought of America as a nation at all. We were then thirteen separate colonies sharing hardly anything besides the English language, and even then speaking it with different accents. Each region had its own culture, its own economy, its own self-interest. The Carolinas kept closer touch with England than with New England. When Ben Franklin spoke of his "country," he meant Boston.

What ostensibly brought the colonies together was panic over paper. The British Parliament passed the Stamp Act in 1765, decreeing that any kind of paper had to carry stamps like those still seen on cigarette packs today. The colonies practically ran on paper—everything from newspapers, pamphlets, and books to legal forms, invoices, and advertisements. This would have been a great source of revenue to cover the costs of the war that Britain had just waged on American soil with the French and Indians.

The colonists reacted to this threat to their prosperity with vigor. To them, it was taxation without their consent. They refused to pay the new stamp tax, punished anyone who did, harassed the tax collectors, stepped up smuggling activities along the coasts, and organized a boycott that made London merchants lobby Parliament to repeal the law. The organizers behind all this radical activity became national heroes before there was a nation.

Calling themselves "Sons of Liberty," by which they meant economic liberty, these radicals were groups of reputable merchants and professionals in major port cities who met in secret to maintain anonymity. Chapters in various colonies would communicate by means of committees of correspondence, planning and plotting such activities as the intercolonial boycott that finally forced repeal of the Stamp

3

Act in March of 1766. As soon as celebration over that repeal died down so did zeal for united action.

Pursuit of each colony's self-interest had been encouraged by the government's earlier policy of "benign neglect," allowing them to flourish by leaving them alone. Now, however, in seeking some way to pay for defending the colonies, the British authorities tightened up security against American smuggling and sought to protect their customs collectors. In New England especially this led to action-and-reaction cycles which inevitably brought bloodshed, recrimination, and ultimately insurrection.

The notorious Boston Massacre provides a ready instance. British troops sent to the city to guard the customs officers had to supplement meager pay by moonlighting, thereby taking jobs away from local men and in many instances fraternizing with local girls. Street fights between soldiers and citizens became routine. Gangs of idle, sometimes unemployed and homeless men and boys who prowled the streets at night, only added to the unrest. In early March of 1770 a mob attacked a sentry guarding the Custom House, and were repulsed by British reinforcements, who panicked and fired wildly into the crowd, killing three and fatally wounding two others. At their later trial, a local jury found the soldiers had fired in self defense, but the loss of American life was exploited for propaganda by such patriots as Paul Revere. Circulated in the popular press and as a broadside, (a single sheet pasted up on public walls like a poster), his celebrated engraving of the Boston Massacre did little more for united action than make Americans mad.

If loss of life would not move Americans enough, neither did loss of civil rights. When Rhode Island smugglers, among them many reputable merchants active in the Sons of Liberty, burned the British revenue ship *Gaspee* in 1772, colonial authorities knew that no local jury would convict the culprits and wanted to send them to England for trial. This was a clear violation of the British Constitution going back to the Magna Carta. From the earliest days, British settlers in the New World had been promised full privileges of citizenship, and now both the Constitution and colonial charters were being violated. Yet the ties to England of economic wellbeing, custom, and family were so strong not even this moved the Americans to united action.

Slowly, New England Sons of Liberty increased their pressure until the celebrated Boston Tea Party of December 1773, when they dumped British tea into Boston harbor rather than pay the tax on it. British authorities irately demanded reparations and, when the Americans refused, closed the port of Boston to further commerce. This time, colonists reacted to the threat to economic liberty. Even George Washington, who seldom spoke in public, is said to have offered to raise an army and march at its head to Boston's relief. Using the Sons of Liberty corresponding committees, news raced from colony to colony, urging mutual support of their Boston brethren. What patriotic Americans could do less?

SEEING THE
LIBERTY TREE

Solomon Drowne, age 14
Newport, Rhode Island, 1767

*O*n *his trip from Providence to Newport, which took sixteen hours to complete, Solomon saw a good picture of the American colonies on the eve of the Revolution. Before him was a lush prosperity based on trade with the West Indies that included privateering and smuggling. At a time when Haiti alone had more trade than the thirteen colonies combined, the islands still depended on the mainland colonies for food and investments in ships and shipping. Newport's harbor made it ideal for a person like Colonel Gregory Malbone, whose fleet of privateers ranged the world, to plunder any ship flying a foreign flag while his smaller boats smuggled imports under cover of darkness to avoid paying taxes at home. Young Solomon marvels at the ruins of Malbone's palatial mansion, burned down the previous year while the tycoon insisted on finishing that day's banquet. The common folk, as Solomon noted, did their banqueting on huge turtles from nearby* *waterways, barbequed in community feasts and washed down with bowls of rum punch, the rum imported from the West Indies untaxed. Both business and pleasure were led by groups of merchants and workmen alike, banded in secret societies called Sons of Liberty to agitate for freedom from British controls. Just a couple of years earlier, their protests had gained repeal of the hated Stamp Act. Their liberty poles flew flags picturing the liberty tree under which they met or else their liberty symbol of thirteen stripes, alternating red and white. Solomon visited the plaque commemorating their victory. And he also visits the local graveyard which had headstones so old they gave evidence of how deep these Americans had planted roots in the New World.*

June 23. My father and I set out for Newport in Rhode Island. We stepped aboard the packet boat, Thomas Lynsey, Commander-in-chief, at about 8 o'clock in the morning. We sailed as far as Sassafras Point, then spoke with a sloop from Newport bound for Providence, Captain Jackson, Commander. We sailed as far as Bristol. Then with a merry trumpet spoke with a schooner from Saint Kitts bound for Providence, Captain Burroughs, Commander. We saw William Gladding's windmill and the church steeple. We had a very bad time, for the wind was ahead, and tide, and were forced to run four miles in a tack to gain half a mile.

When we came at Portsmouth, Rhode Island, I was very seasick. . . . I was asleep when we first came to the wharf, which was about 12 o'clock at night. A very poor voyage indeed for thirty miles.

June 24. The next morning we went up in the street where we could see from the Liberty Tree to the lower end of the town. First walked over to the point to Elisha Clarke's house.

There we saw a Liberty Pole where they hoist the flag. From thence we advanced down to Mrs. Extine's and ate breakfast. From thence we went up the hill, where we saw windmills enough. I was sick there for awhile.

Then we came down to the Court House. We went into the Court House, went up chamber, in a room, where we saw several pictures amongst which stood "Liberty, the Daughter of Heaven," and our sovereign, George the Third [who was giving his consent to the repeal of the Stamp Act], and other great men.

We took a walk uptown to Liberty Tree, on which was a plate with these letters in gold:

THE TREE OF LIBERTY

M.DCC.LXV

The Stamp Act Repealed

MARCH XVIII. M.DCC.LXVI.

We went up to the town burying place where we saw many graves and tombs. There was one 100 years old we saw there, dated 1667. Very old was the tombs. We could hardly observe the figures [on the headstones].

We went up to Captain Laten's, where we got a bowl of punch. There was a turtle frolic at his house the same day. The turtle's weight was above 200 pounds. From his house we went down to the beach. There we saw the raging of the seas from the ocean. We looked before us and could see no land, nothing but sea and sky. We saw a vessel which looked as small as a mountain and as large as a little canoe. There we saw the gallows where [pirate John] Shearman was hung upon the beach. We got large clam shells on the shore. We saw negroes dressing fish in great plenty to barrel, for there were large piles upon the shore. We came from thence up towards town and saw four windmills agoing and one astanding still.

We saw Mr. Redwood's garden—one of the finest gardens I ever saw in my life. In it grows all sorts of West India fruit, viz.: oranges, lemons, limes, pineapples, tamarinds, and other sorts. It also has West India flowers—very pretty ones—and a fine summer house. It was told my father by a credible person that the garden was worth 40,000 pounds and that the man that takes care of the garden has above 100 dollars per annum. It has hothouses where things that are tender are put in the winter, and hot beds for the West India fruit. I saw one or two gardens in coming from the beach.

June 25. Lewis Jenkins and I went up to Colonel Malbone's house—or the ruins of his house. There was a fine garden and summer house. There his house was built of stone and, marvel! had six chimneys. In his garden was a fish pond and a duck pond. The water was drawn out of the fish pond when his house was burnt. So we came home to Mrs. Extine's. We got our things in readiness and set out for home at forty minutes after twelve o'clock. We had a fair wind for us and tide. I felt seasick a little as we were coming home. We got home at about fourteen minutes before four o'clock in the afternoon.

—"Dr. Solomon Drowne's Journal,"
Newport Historical Magazine
1 (October 1980): 65–68.

TESTIFYING AT THE
BOSTON MASSACRE TRIAL

Slave Andrew, age 20?
Boston, 1770

*T*hree things surprise modern readers about Andrew's testimony
for the evening of March 5, 1770, when British soldiers fired on
citizens of Boston. First, that a slave's testimony would be accepted
in court. In a Massachusetts court, the fact that Andrew was a slave
was irrelevant. More important was his credibility. His owner,
respected merchant Oliver Wendell, testified that Andrew could read
and write, and never told a lie. As a member of the Sons of Liberty,
Wendell had nothing at all to gain from shading the truth although
he did call Andrew "highly imaginative." Nonetheless, both prosecution lawyers and the judge said Andrew's was the clearest testimony
in the soldiers' trial.

The second surprise in reading Andrew's testimony is how different the facts are from what many of us have been taught about the
Boston Massacre. The biggest difference is that the British soldiers did

not attack the American mob. Rather, they were the victims of mob violence. The trouble began when about twenty teenaged boys started throwing snowballs at a lone sentry outside the Custom House. Joined by six more soldiers, a corporal, and their captain, the British tried to make their way back to their quarters through a barrage of rocks, snowballs, and rocks-in-snowballs. The initial shot was fired when trooper Hugh Montgomery's gun was knocked from his hands, hit the ground, and discharged, setting off a panic that Andrew describes. Our misunderstanding of what really happened is a direct result of Paul Revere's famous engraving of the event, which was deliberately printed as pure propaganda: even the soldiers' uniforms are not accurately portrayed.

The third surprise is that the jury believed Andrew's testimony and found the soldiers not guilty of murder although two had their thumbs branded with the letter "M" for manslaughter in self-defense. Ironically, the five American dead included Crispus Attucks, himself a slave and the first to fall.

Although Andrew faded out of history, the Revere engraving lived on. It was even put on the backs of bills, so together with the broadsides published on the Boston Massacre, and versions circulated through the Sons of Liberty network, that one picture made its way out of the city into the countryside where it incensed Americans as nothing had done before, not even the Stamp Act. Chances are, only a few people ever saw the more accurate portrayal given in court by Slave Andrew.

☆ ☆ ☆

On the evening of the fifth of March I was at home. I heard the bells ring and went to the gate. I stayed there a little and saw Mr. Lovell coming back with his buckets. I asked him where was the fire. He said it was not fire.

After that, I went into the street and saw one of my

acquaintances coming up . . . holding his arm. I asked him, "What's the matter?"

He said the soldiers were fighting, had got cutlasses, and were killing everybody, and that one of them had struck him on the arm and almost cut it off. He told me I had best not go down.

I said a good club was better than a cutlass, and he had better go down and see if he could not cut some [soldiers], too.

I went to the Town House, saw the sentinels. Numbers of boys on the other side of the way were throwing snowballs at them. The sentinels were enraged and swearing at the boys. The boys called them, "Lobsters, bloody backs," and hollered, "Who buys lobsters!"

One of my acquaintance came and told me that the soldiers had been fighting, and the people had drove them to Murray's barracks. I saw a number of people coming from Murray's barracks who went down by Jackson's corner into King Street.

Presently I heard three cheers given in King Street. I said, "We had better go down and see what's the matter." We went down to the whipping post and stood by Waldo's shop. I saw a number of people 'round the sentinel at the Custom House.

There were also a number of people who stood where I did and were picking up pieces of sea coal that had been thrown out thereabout and snowballs, and throwing them over at the sentinel. While I was standing there, there were two or three boys run out from among the people and cried, "We have got his gun away and now we will have him!"

Presently I heard three cheers given by the people at the Custom House. I said to my acquaintance I would run up and see whether the guard would turn out. I passed round the guard house and went as far as the west door of the Town House.

I saw a file of men, with an officer with a laced hat on before them. Upon that, we all went to go towards him, and when we had got about half way to them, the officer said something to them, and they filed off down the street.

Upon that, I went in the shadow towards the guard house and followed them down as far as Mr. Peck's corner. I saw them pass through the crowd and plant themselves by the Custom House. As soon as they got there, the people gave three cheers.

I went to cross over to where the soldiers were and as soon as I got a glimpse of them, I heard somebody huzza and say, "Here is old Murray [Justice-of-the-Peace] with the riot act"— and they began to pelt snowballs.

A man set out and run, and I followed him as far as Philips's corner, and I do not know where he went. I turned back and went through the people until I got to the head of Royal Exchange Lane right against the soldiers. The first word I heard was a grenadier say to a man by me, "Damn you, stand back."

Question. How near was he to him?

Answer. He was so near that the grenadier might have run him through if he had stepped one step forward. While I stopped to look at him, a person came to get through betwixt the grenadier and me, and the soldier had like to have pricked him [with the sword]. He turned about and said, "You damned lobster, bloody back, are you going to stab me?"

The soldier said, "By God, will I!"

Presently somebody took hold of me by the shoulder and told me to go home or I should be hurt. At the same time there were a number of people towards the Town House who said, "Come away and let the guard alone. You have nothing at all to do with them."

I turned about and saw the officer standing before the men, and one or two persons engaged in talk with him. A number were jumping on the backs of those that were talking with the officer, to get as near as they could.

Question. Did you hear what they said?

Answer. No. Upon this, I went to go as close to the officer as I could. One of the persons who was talking with the officer turned about quick to the people and said, "Damn him, he is going to fire!" Upon that, they cried out, "Fire and be damned, who cares! Damn you, you dare not fire," and began to throw snowballs and other things, which then flew pretty thick.

Question. Did they hit any of them?

Answer. Yes, I saw two or three of them hit. One struck a grenadier on the hat. And the people who were right before them had sticks, and as the soldiers were pushing their guns back and forth, they struck their guns, and one hit a grenadier on the fingers.

At this time, the people up at the Town House called again, "Come away! Come away!" A stout man who stood near me and right before the grenadiers as they pushed with their bayonets the length of their arms, kept striking on their guns.

The people seemed to be leaving the soldiers and to turn from them when there came down a number from Jackson's corner huzzaing and crying, "Damn them, they dare not fire!" "We are not afraid of them!"

One of these people, a stout man [Crispus Attucks] with a long cordwood stick, threw himself in and made a blow at the officer. I saw the officer try to fend off the stroke. Whether he struck him or not, I do not know. The stout man then turned round and struck the grenadier's gun at the Captain's right hand and immediately fell in with his club and knocked his gun away and struck him over the head. The blow came either on the soldier's cheek or hat.

This stout man held the bayonet with his left hand and twitched it and cried, "Kill the dogs! Knock them over!" This was the general cry. The people then crowded in and, upon that, the grenadier gave a twitch back and relieved his gun, and he up with it and began to pay away on [shoot at] the people.

I was then betwixt the officer and this grenadier. I turned to go off. When I had got away about the length of a gun, I turned to look towards the officer, and I heard the word, "Fire!" I thought I heard the report of a gun and, upon hearing the report, I saw the same grenadier swing his gun and immediately he discharged it.

Question. Did the soldiers of that party, or any of them, step or move out of the rank in which they stood to push the people?

Answer. No, and if they had they might have killed me and many others with their bayonets.

Question. Did you, as you passed through the people towards Royal Exchange Lane and the party, see a number of people take up any and everything they could find in the street and throw them at the soldiers?

Answer. Yes, I saw ten or fifteen round me do it.

Question. Did you yourself . . . .

Answer. Yes, I did.

Question. After the gun fired, where did you go?

Answer. I run as fast as I could into the first door I saw open . . . I was very much frightened.

—*Trial of William Wemms [et al.],*
Soldiers in His Majesty's 29th Regiment of Foot,
for the Murder of Crispus Attucks [et al.]
(1770): Appendix, 212–16.

BRIBED BY THE
SONS OF LIBERTY

Charles Bourgatte, age 14

Boston, 1770

*A*s *a witness in the Boston Massacre trial, Charles testified that he and his employer had fired at the mob from upstairs windows in the Custom House. Charles was an apprentice clerk to Edward Manwaring, Boston's toughest customs officer, who had only recently been transferred from the Gaspé area of Canada where Charles had been born. Because the boy's English was broken, the judge called in French interpreters to make sure the jury understood what Charles was saying.*

As a mere apprentice, Charles was in a social class on a level with a slave. Apprentices gave up seven years of their lives to serve a master who was supposed to offer vocational training, board, room, clothing, and so on in payment for labor. Often, boys' parents would have to pay a fee besides. Apprentices like Charles had no money of their own and would spend their free time hanging out with other

17

apprentices, making up a good part of mobs like the one at the Massacre. As Charles points out in his testimony, he had to obey his master even if it meant shooting at his pals.

Although Charles insisted that he told the truth, the trial revealed that he had lied, because radical Sons of Liberty led by the notorious William Molineux had bribed him with gingerbread and threatened him with death to implicate his master. The boy was jailed for perjury and sentenced to twenty-five lashes at the whipping post. Only a sad pawn in the power struggle on both sides of the Atlantic, Charles was rescued by Molineux's friends half way through the whipping—only to face the second half a few days later.

☆ ☆ ☆

I am an apprentice to Mr. Edward Manwaring. On the evening of the fifth of March last, I was at Mr. Hudson's in Back Street at the North End, where my master then lodged. Mr. Hudson and his wife were at home. When the bells rung [for the riot], I ran into King Street and to the door of the Custom House, which was on ajar, partly open. And a young man, one Green, he with one eye [pointing to Hammond Green] opened the door and pulled me in.

Two or three gentlemen came downstairs, and one of them, a tall man, pulled me upstairs and said to me, "If you don't fire, I'll kill you." I went upstairs and stood at a front window in the chamber, and the tall man loaded two guns with two balls each, and I fired them both.

As soon as I had fired one gun, he, the tall man, said again to me, "If you don't fire, I will kill you." He had a cane with a sword in it in his hand, and compelled me to fire both the guns. After I had fired these two guns, Mr. Manwaring fired our gun also out of the same window. The tall man loaded the three guns, and I see him put the balls into each of them and heard them go down. The two guns I fired, I pointed up the street and in the air.

When my master, Mr. Manwaring, pointed his gun out of the window I was in the room but went out and was on the stairs before his gun went off. I heard it but did not see it. As soon as I had fired, the tall man took me downstairs and said he would give me money if I would not tell. I replied, I did not want any money but if I was called before the Justices, I would tell the truth.

There were a great many people in the house and a number of people round me in the chamber where I fired. I can't tell the precise number, but there were more than ten. Mr. Munro and Hammond Green were in the house below stairs. Mr. Manwaring was in the chamber when all the three guns were loaded and fired. There was the space of a minute and a half between the second gun I fired and the third which my master fired.

There was a candle in the chamber, but I cannot tell whether there were one or two windows in it. When I came up into the chamber, there were two guns in it. I fired twice out of the same gun, but I cannot tell whether Mr. Manwaring fired the same gun I did. At the time I and my master fired, the street below was full of people and the mob were throwing sticks, snowballs, etc. It was pretty dark, but I don't know but there might be a little moon. I can't tell whether the guns my master and I fired were fired before or after the firing by the soldiers.

When I went from Mr. Hudson's to the Custom House, I passed through the lane that leads from the Market to the Custom House, Royal Exchange Lane, and I did not see the sentry box or any soldiers near the Custom House. There were many people round there in the street. Immediately after

I went downstairs, I went out of the house and saw a great number of people throwing snowballs and sticks, but I saw no soldiers. I returned to Mr. Hudson's house. Mr. Hudson and his wife were then at home, and no other person in the house.

. . .

[*Court Summary*.] Upon being again asked where he was when he heard the report of his master's gun, says he was quite downstairs.

Upon being asked whether he was not soon after his commitment taken out of jail and examined by Mr. Molineux, and that the latter told him to tell the truth and that this was previous to his examination before the Justices.

☆   ☆   ☆

Four witnesses testify that no shots at all came from the Custom House. Elizabeth Avery, resident of the Custom House, then testified that the boy had not been there that fatal night, nor had she ever seen him before he testified in court. His landlady, Mrs. Hudson, then testified he "was not out of her sight five minutes at a time, from the time the bells began until after ten o'clock," nor did Mr. Manwaring or the others leave her house.

Finally, James Penny, who had been jailed for debt, testified that, when in jail, the boy had told him his testimony at the soldiers' trial about firing from the Custom House had been fabricated after William Molineux promised to take care of him and Mrs. Waldron, the gingerbread lady, gave him gingerbread and cheese. Although the boy denied he ever said that, the jury dismissed his story completely.

—*Trial of William Wemms [et al.],*
Soldiers in His Majesty's 29th Regiment of Foot,
for the Murder of Crispus Attucks [et al.]
(1770): Appendix, 212–16.

A BRITISH SCHOOLGIRL
IN BOSTON

Anna Green Winslow, age 12

Boston, 1772

*E**xcept for referring to the Boston Massacre as "the murder of 5th March last," Anna's diary holds few allusions to the growing tension that will lead to war. She makes references to soldiers, but this is to be expected: her father was an army officer stationed in Nova Scotia and her diary consists of letters to the folks back there—mother, father, and two young brothers.*

Direct descendants of the pioneer Puritans, her parents' large families still lived in Boston. Anna stayed with her aunt Sarah Winslow Deming so she could attend the various schools required for "finishing" a proper Bostonian lass—schools for sewing, dancing, and especially writing. The diary is written as part of her writing lessons. That is why it is in the form of letters home. Mostly Anna tells about the sermons she heard and read, but she also gives details of how she would spend her days baking pies, making purses, knitting and spinning, or visiting. At twelve she was old enough to attend the parties she calls "constitutions"—no boys allowed. There the girls would wear the latest fashions in clothes and headdresses as Anna describes in detail. Imitating French fashion, some hairstyles built up with cow or horse hair or wool could reach as high as three feet tall. In effect, Anna provides the equivalent of a modern newspaper's society page even with sophisticated gossip about the housemaid who chases soldiers, burns the jailhouse, and ends up on the gallows.

☆ ☆ ☆

February 25. I have been to writing school this morning and sewing. The day being very pleasant, very little wind stirring. Jemima called to see me last evening. She lives at Master Jimmy Lovel's. Dear Mamma, I suppose that you would be glad to hear that Betty Smith who has given you so much trouble is well and behaves herself well, and I should be glad if I could write you so. But the truth is, no sooner was the 29th Regiment encamped upon the common but Miss Betty took herself among them (as the Irish say) and there she stayed with Bill Pinchion and awhile. The next news of her was that she was got into jail for stealing, from whence she was taken to the public whipping post.

The next adventure was to the Castle after the soldiers were removed there, for the murder of the 5th March last [Boston Massacre]. When they turned her away from there, she came up to town again and soon got into the workhouse for new misdemeanors. She soon ran away from there and set up her old trade of pilfering again, for which she was put a second time into jail. There she still remains.

About two months gone (as well as I can remember) she and a number of her wretched companions set the jail on fire in order to get out, but the fire was timely discovered and extinguished and there, as I said, she still remains till this day in order to be tried for her crimes. I heard somebody say that, as she has some connections with the army, no doubt but she would be cleared and perhaps have a pension into the bargain. Mr. Henry says the way of sin is downhill. When persons get into that way they are not easily stopped. . . .

March 6. I think the appearance this morning is as winterish as any I can remember—earth, houses, trees, all covered with snow, which began to fall yesterday morning and continued falling all last night. The sun now shines very bright, the northwest wind blows very fresh. Mr. Gannett dined here yesterday. From him, my uncle, aunt, and cousin Sally, I had an account of yesterday's public performances and exhibitions [commemorating the Boston Massacre], but Aunt says I need not write about them because, no doubt, there will be printed accounts. I should have been glad if I could have seen and heard for myself. My face is better, but I have got a heavy cold yet.

March 9. After being confined a week I rode yesterday afternoon to and from meeting in Mr. Soley's chaise. I got no cold and am pretty well today. This has been a very snowy day today. Anybody that sees this may see that I have wrote nonsense but Aunt says I have been a very good girl today about my work, however. I think this day's work may be called a piece meal, for in the first place I sewed on the bosom of Uncle's shirt, mended two pairs of gloves, mended for the wash two handkerchiefs (one cambric), sewed on half a border of a lawn apron of Aunt's, read part of the 21st chapter of *Exodus*, and a story in the *Mother's Gift.*

Now, honored Mamma, I must tell you of something that happened before this great while, viz., my Uncle and Aunt both told me I was a very good girl. Mr. Gannett [our headmaster] gave us the favor of his company a little while this morning. I have been writing all the above gibberish while Aunt has been looking after her family. Now she is out of the room—now she is in—and takes up my pen in *my* absence to observe, I am a little simpleton for informing my mamma that it is *a great while* since I was praised, because she will conclude that it is *a great while* since I deserved to be praised. I will henceforth try to observe their praise and yours too. I mean deserve. It's now tea time. As soon as that is over, I shall spend the rest of the evening in reading to my aunt. It is near candle lighting.

April 9. Yesterday afternoon I visited Miss Polly Deming and took her with me to Mr. Rogers's in the evening where Mr. Hunt discoursed upon the seventh question of the catechism, viz., "What are the decrees of God?" I remember a good many of his observations, which I have got set down on a loose paper. But my aunt says that a Miss of 12 years old can't possibly do justice to the nicest subject in Divinity and therefore had better not attempt a repetition of particulars that she finds lie (as may be easily concluded) somewhat confused in my young mind.

My Papa informed me in his last letter that he had done me the honor to read my journals and that he approved of some part of them. I suppose he means that he likes some parts better than others. Indeed it would be wonderful, as Aunt says, if a gentleman of Papa's understanding and judgment could be highly entertained with *every little* saying or observation that came from a girl of my years and that I ought to esteem it a great favor that he notices any of my simple matter with his *approbation*.

April 13. Yesterday I walked to meeting all day, the ground very dry, and when I came home from meeting in the afternoon, the dust blew so that it almost put my eyes out. What a difference in the space of a week. I was just going out to writing school but a slight rain prevented, so Aunt says I must make up by writing at home. Since I have been writing, the rain is turned to snow, which is now falling in a thick shower. I have now before me, honored Mamma, your favor dated January 3. I am glad you altered your mind when you at first thought not to write to me. I am glad my brother made an essay for a postscript to your letter. I must get him to read it to me when he comes up, for two reasons: the one is because I may have the pleasure of hearing his voice, the other because I don't understand his writing. I observe that he is Mamma's "Ducky Darling."

April 17. You see, Mamma, I comply with your orders (or at least have done Father's some time past) of writing in my journal every day, though my matters are of little importance and I have nothing at present to communicate except that I spent yesterday afternoon and evening at Mr. Soley's. The day was very rainy. I hope I shall at least learn to spell the word *yesterday*, it having occurred so frequently in these pages! (The bell is ringing for Good Friday). . . .

May 16. Last Wednesday Bet Smith was set upon the gallows. She behaved with great impudence. Thursday I danced a minuet and country dances at school, after which I drank tea with Aunt Storer. Today I am somewhat out of sorts, a little sick at my stomach.

May 25. Nothing remarkable since the preceding date. Whenever I have omitted a school my aunt has directed me to set it down here, so when you don't see a memorandum of that kind, you may conclude that I have paid my compliments to Messers Holbrook (writing) and Turner (dancing)—to the former, you see, to very little purpose. . . . I had my headroll on. Aunt Storer said it ought to be made less. Aunt Deming said it ought not to be made at all. It makes my head itch and ache and burn like anything, Mamma. This famous roll is not made *wholly* of a red *Cow's Tail* but is a mixture of that and horsehair (very coarse) and a little human hair of yellow hue that I suppose was taken out of the back part of an old wig. But D——— made it (our hair) all carded together and twisted up. When it first came home, Aunt put it on and my new cap on it. She then took up her apron and measured me, and from the top of my notions, I measured above an inch longer than I did downwards from the roots of my hair to the end of my chin. Nothing renders a young person more amiable than virtue and modesty without the help of false hair, red cow tail, or D——— [the barber].

Now all this, Mamma, I have just been reading over to my aunt. She is pleased with my whimsical description and grave (half grave) improvement and hopes a little false English will not spoil the whole day with Mamma. Rome was not built in a day.

—Alice Morse Earle, ed.
Diary of Anna Green Winslow
(Boston: Houghton Mifflin, 1894), 36–72.

TO WED OR
NOT TO WED

Jemima Condict, age 19
Essex County, N.J., 1774–75

*S*aucy *and smart, Jemima left, with her diary, one of the best weapons against a stereotyped view of young persons in her era as being delicate or dull lumps of clay. A farmer's daughter in the lush country northwest of Newark, she must have worked very hard by day, but at night in writing her diary she relived the fun parts, too, and some of those appear in the excerpt here. These reveal a well-rounded person who is confident in society, but less so in her emotions, even bursting into verse as her feelings overflow. She covers her inner conflict with laughter and sometimes self-mockery, but the tension shows. She can be funny when talking about her suitors, or newlyweds like "Bouncer Joan," but she is anxious about the love affair with her cousin, Aaron Harrison, undecided whether marrying a cousin would be okay socially and morally. While her relationship with her mother was loving and respectful, she puts up a good front when others tease* *her about marrying, exchanging put-ons and put-downs expertly, as at the dentist's place. She covers that visit with a laugh, though in those days when everyone had rotten teeth it meant pulling them with pliers and no novocaine. George Washington had to wear dentures of ivory (not wood) so heavy they gave him a permanent scowl. Jemima dismisses the discomfort just as, at first, she dismisses the Boston Tea Party as trivial. When that act of dumping tea into the harbor rather than paying tax on it leads to war, she becomes gradually concerned about her friends who on "training day" learn how to be soldiers, then eagerly march off, some never to return. She does not joke about them.*

☆   ☆   ☆

August 24. This day I am entering another year. I hope I may live and spend it better than I did the last or any that is past. There seems to be a great alteration among the young people this year. Some that was before bad enough is now, I hope, become new creatures. What! and am I still going on in sin, growing worse instead of better? What reason have I to be ashamed?

October 1. It seems we have troublesome times acoming, for there is great disturbance abroad in the earth, and they say it is tea that caused it. So then, if they will quarrel about such a trifling thing as that, what must we expect but war? And I think, or at least fear, it will be so. . . .

October 15. Monday is come and the Lord in His goodness has spared me to see it, I being all the first part of this week very much 'toxicated in my mind about that affair [whether to wed her cousin], for I don't know what to do.

> But boast not, mistaken swain, of thy art
> To please my partial eyes;

The charms that have subdued my heart
Another may despise.

October 20. Spent the whole afternoon with my friends that came from the West Branch, and I heard them tell so much about it that I long to see it. They been at me to go up with them and stay there this winter. I told them if it was but a day's journey I would go but I could not bear the thoughts of going so far from my father's house. They told me there was young men plenty there for me, but I thought I was in no hurry for a husband at present. And if I was, I thought it was too far to go upon uncertainties. So I concluded to stay where I was, and I believe I shan't repent it. A husband or not, I am best off in this spot. But they are going, and I must now take my leave of them—and I don't know but for the last time, so I wished them well.

October 27. I had some discourse with Mr. Chandler. He asked me why I did not marry. I told him I wasn't in no hurry. "Well," said he, "I wish I was married to you." I told him he would soon wish himself unmarried again. "Why so?" "Because," says I, "you will find that I am a cross, ill-contrived piece of stuff." I told him that I would advise all the men to remain as they was, for the women was bad and the men so much worse that it was a wonder if they agreed. So I scared the poor fellow and he is gone.

October 30. I spent this evening in writing, but the worst of it is, what I write is nonsense. If I did but write what would be instructive or that would do me any good or anyone else, 'twould be some sense in spending time and paper. But no wonder I can't write nothing that's good, for I don't do anything that's good. I hope I may live to spend my time better and have better employment for my pen, for I must be scribbling in leisure time. Too, I find but very little time now. Sometimes after our people is gone to bed, I get my pen, for I don't know how to content myself without writing something.

1775

February 7. Being full of thoughts about What to Do, as I have this year past. Sometimes I think I will certain bid him [her cousin] farewell forever, but I thought I would talk to my mother and see if I could be convinced one way or t'other, for I want to hear the grounds of what they have to say. So one day my mother says to me, "Your father is going to get you a [hope] chest." I told her I should be glad of one but would not have her think 'twas because I thought to marry. "Why," says she, "don't you never intend to marry?" I told her, people said I was agoing to have Mr.———[Harrison]. But they tell me they don't think it is a right thing, and it is forbid, etc. But can't none of them, as I can find out, tell me where 'tis forbid [in the Bible]. "So," says I, "what do you think of it, mother?" She said she did not think it was right except I thought it was myself. I asked her if she thought my thinking it was right would make it so. She said my thinking so would cause a contented, easy mind.

"Well," says I, "but that ain't telling what you think about it." She said she had heard his mother talk about it and was against his coming here. She said moreover that she was apt to think I would live a dog's life amongst them. This made me think I would not have him, but I still insisted upon hearing what she had to say.

At last she told me that she had thought a great deal about it, and for her part could not see but that it was right. And as for its being forbid, she did not think there was such a place in the Bible. She said likewise that she did not see what ministers should marry them for if 'twas forbid. So, after this and much more being said, I turned it off with a laugh and said, "What a fool am I! I talk as if I was going to marry a cousin in good earnest but did not know as I had one that would have me." But if I hold my tongue and say nothing, others will have all the talk. They talk to me but convince they don't. I could wish with all my heart I knew the right way and could be made to choose it. If it be wrong, then what a fool was I while young to place my mind on such a one as a cousin, it's very true. It's "O, poor me, what shall I do?" Why, I tell you what a conclusion I made and hope I may hold to it and that is to trust in Him who knows all things, for He knows what is best for me and what I ought to do and what I ought not to do.

February 13. Tuesday. Went up to my sister Ogden's and there was a house full of people, and we had a great sing indeed, for the Horse Neck-ites and the Newark-ites were both assembled together, and there was a new married couple, L. W., Jr., and you may be sure they cut a fine figure, for she is a Bouncer Joan and he a little cross, snipper-snapper snipe. They tell me he cried when he was married, at which I don't a bit wonder for I think 'twas enough to make the poor fellow bellow if he had his wits about him, for I'm sure she can beat him. I don't know. Though he is, like shorn roast pork, more strengthenin', his wife said that shorner was better, as she was. But, then, he was more strengthenin', so I will leave them to make the best of their bargain. I don't know as anyone has lost, for she had a doleful long nose and he a conceived [cleft] chin like myself.

February 17. Resolved if possible to have my tooth out, so down I went to Dr. C. and he got his cold iron ready. My tooth was easy, and I told him I dast not venture. I knew he'd hurt but I could not make him promise he would not, though I thought he began to pity me a little, and that was what I did it for; for it's true, I believe I wasn't so afraid as I pretended to be. I was in hopes he'd draw it easier for it, and I don't know but he did, for he was mighty careful. But when he put his contrivance in my mouth, I pulled them out again. At last they fell alaughing at me and said if I dast not have a tooth drawed I never would be fit to marry. I told them I never reckoned to be if it was as bad as to have a tooth drawed, at which they all fell alaughing, for I was fool for them. But it wa'nt long before I could put my tooth in my pocket and laugh with the best of them.

Yesterday. Mr. ———— come again and wanted me to go with him to Elizabethtown. I made several excuses, for I was resolved not to go. But he would hear to none of them. At last I told him mother would not let me go, so I winked to her to say no, for she was present. So she told him it would not do. Then he fell to coaxing her, but she said, "No, I won't let her go." So he went off gentleman-like, but I thought when he got upon his little nag, though, he did not need a page boy riding with him for he almost covered the nag by himself [because of his bulk]. But he has gone off, and I believe he's mad withal, but I can't help it now.

Monday. Monday, which was called training day, I rode with my dear father down to see them train, there being several companies met together. I thought it would be a mournful sight to see if they had been fighting in earnest and how soon they will be called forth to the field of war we cannot tell, for by what we can hear, the quarrels are not likely to be made up without bloodshed. I have just now heard say that all hopes of conciliation between Britain and her colonies are at an end, for both the King and his parliament have announced our destruction. Fleet and armies are preparing with utmost diligence for that purpose.

April 23. As every day brings new troubles, so this day brings news that yesterday very early in the morning they began to fight at Boston. The regulars we hear shot first there. They killed 30 of our men, 150 of the regulars.

April 30. This day I think is a day of mourning. We have word come that the [British] fleet is coming into New York also and today the men of our town is to have a general meeting to conclude upon measures which may be most proper to be taken. They have chose men to act for them, and I hope the Lord will give them wisdom to conduct wisely and prudently in all matters. . . .

—*Jemima Condict, Her Book*
(Newark, N.J.: Carteret Book Club, 1930), 36–52.

Part II
☆ ☆ ☆
Fighting for Freedom

1775–1778

As soon as the British closed Boston port, Sons of Liberty organized mass protests in other colonies and, of course, in towns and villages throughout New England, an important step inasmuch as radical activity had been limited to cities and larger towns. Now the merchants and the townspeople were joined by farmers and frontiersmen mutually outraged.

New England villagers, especially, started collecting arms and ammunition (some stolen from British arsenals), hiding them under churches and in barns. The British knew what was going on and sent squads of soldiers into the countryside to recover both what had been stolen and what the farmers owned. This was particularly threatening to farmers and frontiersmen who depended on guns to put meat on the table.

That is why the troops who sought arms and ammunition in Lexington and Concord villages in April 1775 met such strong resistance. The aptly named Minutemen (and Minute-women, who shot from kitchen windows) forced the troops back to Boston, penning them up in the city and besieging them from surrounding hills.

Americans had cracked the myth of British invincibility. The committees of correspondence were quick to transmit body counts—the seasoned British troops had lost 250 men. Worse, they had fired on women and children: they had fired on a woman standing between husband and father firing a blunderbuss from their window. The redcoated grenadiers killed all three along with the baby of the house.

That is the kind of report which ignited enlistments for the Continental army now gathering under General George Washington's command at nearby Cambridge. It soon numbered 5,000, not counting such likeminded troops as Ethan Allen's Green Mountain Boys, who captured needed arms and ammunition from British forts on Lake Champlain. The

June 1775 reinforced British assault on Breed's Hill, or nearby Bunker Hill, outside Boston, took a terrible toll of Americans and the large number of bodies in one small space only added to the misery on both sides.

Refugees from the surrounding towns streamed into the Boston area to escape further gunfire. With no sanitary facilities worthy of the name, they all lived in dirt and depression, destitute of money or morale, with a limited food supply. Civilians and soldiers alike fell to ravages of typhus, typhoid, cholera, and yellow fever. Influenza especially took its heavy toll. In Boston alone a quarter of the deaths were from smallpox. One in six who survived that dreaded disease suffered lifelong disfigurement from the pockmarks. General Washington himself feared this only less than dysentery, or "camp fever," which accounted for more debility and death than any other disease and which, in fact, carried off his only stepson.

Bolstered by mercenary Hessian troops, the British evacuated Boston in March 1776. The Americans tried skirmishes around New York City without success and began a waiting game to see who would tire first. They assumed the role of guerillas, harassing the British troops and supplies as the British pushed forward to occupy the colonial capital, Philadelphia.

The fighting spread to the sea. American skippers with skills sharpened by smuggling formed an impromptu navy, capturing British supply ships, distributing the cargoes to beleagured Yanks. Some had been pirates, sharing with their crews whatever booty they could capture on the high seas. Now they all became privateers, manning their private vessels in the service of their respective local governments. Their swift ships made it possible for Ben Franklin in London as agent for Massachusetts to learn of the Bunker Hill battle even before George III knew of it.

Most important, King George III now became the colonists' chief antagonist, a role previously restricted to Parliament or his cabinet ministers. Tom Paine's *Common Sense* had appeared in January 1776, asserting that the King was responsible for all their problems and had to go: monarchy itself had lived past its time; the Age of Human Equality had arrived; and America's cause was "in great measure the cause of all mankind." Paine articulated the reason to rebel, justifying the morality of breaking the oath all citizens had sworn to be loyal to King George III.

When Thomas Jefferson drafted the Declaration of Independence in July of 1776, he already had the precedent of a resolution by Congress a month earlier declaring the colonies independent. Jefferson's document took the form of a legal indictment, spelling out for other nations the legitimate claims the colonies made against the King's abuse of their natural rights. Even more clearly than Paine had done in *Common Sense*, Jefferson asserted the secular creed for Americans ever after: "All men are created equal."

Meanwhile, October 1777 brought about an event that changed the course of the occupation and the Revolution itself. This was the defeat of General "Gentleman Johnny" Burgoyne in upstate New York. He was supposed to move down from Canada to join forces with the other British troops in Philadelphia, which would have meant utter defeat for the Americans. But, using tactics better fit for European warfare, harassed by American guerillas, and completely underestimating his needs, he ran out of supplies and surrendered his army at Saratoga. His defeat persuaded France to trust American fighting power and so they furnished arms, ammunition, and men to help win the war.

SURVIVING
BUNKER HILL

Samuel Webb, age 19
Cambridge, Mass., 1775

S̸am Webb could see the outbreak of fighting from two points of view. He was secretary to his stepfather, Silas Deane, a member of the First Continental Congress. At the same time, Sam was a lieutenant in Connecticut's militia, the national guard of its day. As secretary he had to keep his stepfather informed at all times, for this was the way Congress and the patriots knew what was going on as the colonies began to unite for full scale war. As an officer he saw the impact of the situation in military terms—the prospect of death and dying, the need for strategic defense, and for unity among forces from various colonies under the newly-appointed commander-in-chief, George Washington.

The first letter here betrays Sam's worries about his sister Sarah in late 1774. Married to a Boston Tory, she had found her front door smeared with blood—clearly an act of vandalism. Sam's fears of mob violence were very real: radical Sons of Liberty and genuine idle or criminal elements had become indistinguishable at times. The unrest in the colonies had intensified and many used that as a pretext for lawlessness.

In the next two letters Sam describes the fighting that took place on a hill overlooking Boston harbor just eight months later. Much had happened. To protest the shutting down of the port of Boston by the British in June 1774, the colonies had convened the First Continental Congress in Philadelphia. Their agreement that the British government's actions were "unconstitutional, dangerous, and destructive" led to the banning of arms, ammunition, and militias by British General Thomas Gage, acting governor of Boston. It was downhill from there: acts of theft, boycott, and sabotage by the patriots produced severe British reactions, such as restraints on trade and fishing rights. Rumors flew of religious suppression, more taxes, even imminent British massacre and open patriotic rebellion. The battles of Lexington and Concord, April 19, 1775, brought the situation to the edge. Although Britain offered conciliation in the form of freedom from taxation to any colony willing to govern itself, and the Congress went on debating whether to negotiate or petition for redress of grievances, the battle at Bunker Hill blasted any chance of taking either route.

Thinking they had the British trapped in Boston, the patriots built fortifications and barricades on hills north and south of the city, a half-mile away. Bunker Hill was the higher of the two on the north, but they chose Breed's Hill to defend against what they assumed would be the British attempt to break out of the trap.

On June 17, 1775, 2,000 redcoated infantry and grenadiers commanded by three seasoned generals, Sir William Howe, Henry Clinton, and John Burgoyne, marched up the hill along a half-mile front. Bostonian spectators watched fascinated from steeples, rooftops, and nearby roads as wave after wave of redcoats hammered at the New Englanders at the barricades. The patriot militias, numbering

1,500 men at most, lost a third of their force in two and a half hours of fighting. Sad to report, hundreds of ablebodied men watched from safety the whole time, without offering to help. The beginnings of the war were not clear to all people; families were divided in their sentiments, and many were scornful, or frightened, or simply undecided where their loyalties lay. The slaughter on both sides was awful, and with Bunker Hill, the hope of peace was lost.

☆ ☆ ☆

From a letter to his stepfather Silas Deane.

October 10, 1774. From Wethersfield, Conn. My continual uneasiness and anxiety on account of my sisters who are now in Boston has determined me to pay them a visit, and if some unforeseen incident does not prevent, I intend setting off the last of this week, shall take Newport, Providence, etc., in my way and will, if anything new or interesting, write you from each place but more particularly from the present seat of noise and confusion, say Boston, the true situation of it and fortifications which are now erecting at the only entrance of that large capital.

My brother seems more at ease about our sister than *you*, by your letter, or *I* do. May all his conjectures be right. That "they [are] as safe there as here," is my most fervent wish, but much I fear. On the first hostility, such as blood shed by the troops in Boston, this [Connecticut] colony will most undoubtedly be immediately under arms and march for Boston. The Light Infantry at Middletown, to which I two years belonged, have now a very fine stand of arms, which I purchased for them in New York on my return home from Philadelphia. They have given me an invitation to make one of the number, should any emergency call their appearance in the field, which with my whole heart I shall readily accept if occasion [demands]. But heaven forbid we may ever arrive to this unhappy crisis! But all have drawn their arms, and myself among the rest.

Mobs, which I fancy you judge ruinous to all good government, will be opposed by every true Son of Liberty in this Colony. Other methods may be adopted more effectual to still our *very few* remaining enemies. A reason and I think a very good one is given, that all such riots should be stopped in their first growth, viz.: "A day may come, and in all probability soon will, unless a redress of our grievances can be obtained, that we may be as destitute of all law and Civil Government as the Massachusetts now is. Then, if mobs are allowed to take hold of persons and private property, dissensions will follow, and we soon should be, instead of a United, a broken Body." These are the principles our warmest friends adopt and, as I before hinted, I think good.

From a letter to his brother Joseph,
reporting action on Bunker Hill, 1775.

June 19. After the alarm, on our march down we met many of our worthy friends wounded, sweltering in their blood, carried on the shoulders of their fellow soldiers. Judge you what must be our feelings at this shocking spectacle. The orders were, "Press on, press on, our brethren are suffering and will soon be cut off." We pushed on and came into the field of battle.

Through the cannonading of the ships, bombs, chain shot, ring shot, and double-headed shot flew as thick as hail stones. But, thank heaven, few of our men suffered by them. But when we mounted the summit where the engagement was, good God how the balls flew! I freely acknowledge I never had such a tremor come over me before.

We descended the hill into the field of battle and began our fire very briskly. The regulars [British soldiers] fell in great plenty but to do them justice they keep a grand front and stood their ground nobly. Twice before this time they gave way, but not long before we saw numbers mounting the walls of our fort—on which our men in the fort were ordered to fire and make a swift retreat.

We covered their retreat till they came up with us by a brisk fire from our small arms. The dead and wounded lay on every side of me. Their groans were piercing indeed, though long before this time, I believe, the fear of death had quitted every breast. They now had possession of our fort and four field pieces and by much the advantage of the ground. And, to tell you the truth, our reinforcements belonging to this province, very few of them came into the field but lay skulking the opposite side of the hill.

Our orders then came to make the best retreat we could. We set off, almost gone with fatigue, and ran very fast up the hill, leaving some of our dead and wounded in the field. We retreated over Charlestown Neck through the thickest of the ships' fire. Here some principal officers fell by cannon and bombs.

After we had got out of the ships' fire under the covert of a hill near another entrenchment of ours, we again rallied and lined every part of the road and fields. Here we were determined to die or conquer if they ventured over the Neck. But it grew dark, and we saw them pitching tents. We retired to our entrenchment and lay on our arms all night, keeping vast numbers of our troops out on scouting parties. They keep up a constant fire from the ships and floating batteries all night, but few of them reached us.

But, alas, how dismal was the sight to see the beautiful and valuable town of Charlestown all in flames. And now behold it a heap of ruins, with nothing standing but a heap of chimneys which, by the by, remains an everlasting monument of British cruelty and barbarity. This battle, though we lost it, cannot but do honor to us, for we fought with less numbers and, though they once or twice almost surrounded the fort, we secured their retreat.

But, alas, in the fort fell some brave fellows, among the unhappy number was our worthy friend Dr. [Joseph] Warren. Alas, he is no more. He fell in his country's cause and fought with the bravery of an ancient Roman. They are in possession of his body and no doubt will rejoice greatly over it. After they entered our fort they mangled the wounded in a most horrid manner by running their bayonets through them and beating their heads to pieces with the breeches of their guns.

In this bloody engagement we have lost Wilson Rowlanson, Roger Fox, Gershom Smith, and Lawrence Sullivan, who we suppose fell—at least their bodies—into the hands of our enemy, their souls we hope in the happy regions of bliss. Wounded: Daniel Deming, Samuel Delling, Epaphras Stevens, and Constant Griswould, none of them mortally. Are in a fair way and likely to recover. To give you the exact number of the whole of our killed and wounded is impossible. Opinions are various and no returns yet made to the Council of War. But the best I can find out is about 120 of our men killed and wounded. Perhaps there may be double that number. I cannot say. A few days and we shall know exactly. Of the regulars I doubt not there are many more lost than of ours. The truth of their numbers 'tis not probable we shall know.

The king's troop to the number of 2 or 3,000 are now encamped on the same hill they were after the battle of Lexington, have twenty field pieces with them and lie under the protection of the ships. Our grand fortification is on Prospect Hill, within a mile and a half of theirs. We have about 3,000 men in it and two 12 pounders, two 9 pounders, two 24 pounders, and six 6 pounders. Here we mean to make a stand.

Should they prove victorious, which heaven forbid, and get possession of this hill, we must retire before them and leave Cambridge to the destruction of those merciless dogs. But heaven, we trust, will appear on our side, and sure I am many thousands of us must fall before we flee from them. [British General Thomas] Gage has said that the 19th of June should be made as memorable as the 19th of April is [the battle of Lexington and Concord]. This is the day, and I assure you we are properly on our guard.

From a letter to his stepfather, Silas Deane.

July 11. Our army are now encamped on Prospect Hill and have got nearly completed our grand breastwork, reaching from the Hill to Mystic River. On our right we have completed several redoubts and breastworks [fortifications] not far distant from each other, so that our lines are now extended from Mystic over to Charles River. The enemy are on Bunker Hill and are not idle. They are fortifying in the strongest manner possible. Their situation is amazingly strong—ten times their number could not rout them. Directly in the front lies the narrow neck of Charlestown, on their right four floating batteries in Mystic River, on their left, next Boston, two ships and several tenders, floating batteries, etc. pointing directly across the Neck—by which it would be almost impossible to pass. We hourly expect them to sally out and attempt to carry [capture] our lines.

I am sorry to say we have not men enough. 'Tis too true. General Washington has desired the Provincial Congress to send in the militia to the number of 4 or 5,000 till we can raise more men. This matter we at present keep a secret for fear our enemies should take advantage of it and make their attack in a number of different places and by that means force our entrenchments. But should they attempt it, 'tis thought by our commander that it will be the most bloody engagement our American world ever knew.

Our men are resolute and determined. On an alarm, of which we have had several within a week, our men seem cheerfully to fly to their alarm posts. We have several thousands of pikes with 12-foot handles, which are placed along our lines and most certainly will be very useful if they attempt to scale the walls. I cannot think but 500 of them at Bunker Hill at time of the battle would have been a means of saving our work. If we had [had the pikes], we must have gained a complete victory, for after landing the [British] troops the boats were all ordered to Boston, that there was no retreat left for them. "Fight, conquer, or die" was what their officers was plainly heard to say very often. Major Bruce, who served two years in Portugal with General Lee, told my brother Joe at the lines that it was the hottest engagement he ever knew, even, says he, the Battle of Minden did not equal it.

For my part I confess, when I was descending into the valley from off Bunker Hill side by side of Captain Chester at the head of our company, I had no more thought of ever rising the Hill again than I had of ascending to heaven as Elijah did, soul and body together. But after we got engaged, to see the dead and wounded around me I had no other feeling but that of revenge. Four men were shot dead within five feet of me, but I thank heaven I escaped with only the graze of a musket ball on my hat.

I think it my duty to tell you the bravery of one of our company. Edward Brown stood side by side with Gershom Smith in the entrenchments. Smith fell. Brown saw his danger, discharged his own and Smith's gun. When they came so close as to push bayonet over our small breastwork, Brown sprang, seized a regular's gun, took it from him, and killed him on the spot, brought off the gun in triumph and has it now by him.

—W. C. Ford, ed.
Correspondence and Journals of Samuel Blachley Webb
(New York: privately printed, 1893),
Vol. 1: 40–43, 64–67 with facsimile, 73–76.

AT YALE IN WARTIME

Elijah Backus, age 17

Connecticut, 1777

*H*istories of Yale make use of Elijah's diary to show how college students lived, but it also shows how they felt about rumors of fighting, disease, and other anxieties. His class of 1777 had fifty-six students, twice the average, so living was twice as hard. Rooms were scarce, rents inflated. Food served in the common dining hall grew scarcer as this worst winter in memory grew colder. Food ran out in December and again in March, forcing the college to shut down and to disperse the students to other sites in Connecticut, following their tutors or, like Elijah and the other seniors, going home. Lodging, as the diary shows, was just as scarce. Some students, in fact, had set fire to the main dormitory while trying to keep warm by burning straw. Firewood was absurdly expensive. Elijah paid the equivalent of $200 in today's money for a load that lasted three weeks!
   Instead of fraternities, Elijah and his friends formed debating

societies to compete with others in the art of declaiming or making speeches, loading them with such Latin tags as "O tempore! O mores!" to impress rather than express their point. In those days, whatever was written was meant to be read aloud, memorized, and declaimed. Students like Elijah made fun out of such documents as the Declaration of Independence, which they knew by heart. And if they could not remember poems, they made up their own.

But all was not fun and games. Elijah's frequent mention of rumors of war reflect his uncertainty about joining the army or staying at Yale. Nobody could be certain about the war: the only news came in letters, often delayed, or in travelers' reports, often distorted by retelling. Similarly, rumors of smallpox epidemics, such as the one which drives Elijah to seek inoculation, could cause widespread panic. Every sixth person who survived would go through life disfigured, some horribly so. Though Elijah notices the flight of carrier pigeons, a plentiful food supply of the time (and now extinct), he mentions nothing of the hunger that closed his college. Though he mentions his father, he barely hints that Backus, senior, was cannon-maker for General Washington's troops. Despite his overall anxiety, which can be seen in his mournful closing poem, Elijah Backus was putting up a good front.

☆　☆　☆

January 8. I am turned out of my lodgings at Mrs. Todd's and am obliged to seek for others. I stopped at Mr. Edwards' last night with Tracy, and am going to live there till I can get another.

January 9. There has happened an eclipse of the sun today, beginning near 9 and lasting till noon.

January 10. There has been an express through town from General Parsons bringing an account that General Washington has had another engagement and has taken 500 more prisoners.

January 11. The right honorable Barnabas Baldwin was here today. Because I did not pay him for the use of his horse he refused to pay me what it cost me for shoeing him, and threatens to go to Tunker [Naphtali Daggett, president of Yale] and complain of me.

January 14. I feel a little off the head today; was not at the recitation at noon and there was none in the afternoon. We have it reported that there has been another engagement, regulars [British soldiers] all killed or taken prisoners and we have all their baggage and 30 field pieces.

January 15. Am rather suspicious that yesterday's story is not trustworthy.

January 16. Hopkins came down last night, and I went to sleep with Hillhouse; have tried today in vain to get a place to live at.

January 17. Bushnell has come down and we can't get a place so we have come to Mrs. Todd's and made up a fire but don't board there.

January 18. It is very cold and I board in the Hall and am very sick with the headache.

January 19. I heard the president preach in the chapel. We hear that Fort Washington is retaken by our troops.

January 20. The yesterday's story is a falsehood. There are 200 prisoners brought into town.

January 21. I have got a load of wood at $2. Bushnell and I have begun to board at Deacon Ball's at 7 shillings a week. I have the constant unhappiness to undergo a series of very disagreeable reflections.

February 1. Today we began the third volume of Locke and I got a quart of rum at Atwater's at 2 shillings a quart.

February 3. Expect to declaim soon. Read arguments today and drank a mug of flip at night.

February 4. Declaimed this morning and plainly showed to the wondering scholars my immense eloquence. . . .

February 11. There is a very dangerous practice in college of those scholars who have had the smallpox going down to see those who are sick with it in town, by which those who have not had it are greatly exposed.

February 15. Bought two loads of wood for 20 shillings. We have an account of a battle in the Jersies in which our people have killed 300 of the enemy.

March 20. It is in my opinion very dangerous living in town on account of the smallpox and 'tis very likely college will be dismissed or removed next week . . . .

March 22. The president has notified the scholars that college will break up next Wednesday in order that they may send for their horses. He further says that when the Corporation come together he will resign his presidentship and has given the scholars an affecting speech, so their tune is turned—for it used to be "old damned Tunker" but now *bona praeses.*

March 28. Cold weather. College was dismissed this A.M. Our horses are not come today.

March 29. The scholars are almost all gone. Mr. Dwight thinks that college won't be called together again in this town, and that our classes won't be called together at all. He has been talking with some of the [senior] class to know their minds, whether if he should call them together in his own name they would be willing to meet at any place he should appoint.

April 1. Bushnell's horse came and he set out about nine. My horse came about 1 P.M. Brother James came to bring it.

The TIMES are
Dreadful,
Dismal,
Doleful,
Dolorous, and
DOLLAR-LESS.

Thursday, *October* 31, 1765.　　THE　　NUMB 1195.

PENNSYLVANIA JOURNAL;
AND
WEEKLY ADVERTISER.

EXPIRING: In Hopes of a Resurrection to LIFE again.

Stamp Act protestors appealed to fear in this scare headline by William Bradford, a leader in Philadelphia's Sons of Liberty and owner of the coffeehouse where they met to plan a boycott of British goods throughout the colonies. 1765.

Bostonians pour taxable tea down the throat of a tax collector, who has been tarred and feathered for the occasion. A liberty tree, as noted in Solomon Drowne's diary, looms behind them—as do colonists dumping tea from a British ship. 1774.

Paul Revere's engraving of the Boston Massacre distorted the facts as reported by Slave Andrew, by making it look like an execution, labeling the Custom House "Butcher's Hall," and even dressing the British soldiers in the wrong uniforms. 1770.

"The Bostonians in Distress" shows other colonists feeding the symbolically imprisoned citizens of Boston in exchange for promises, while they are surrounded by British guns and grenadiers make off with their sheep. While loaded with religious significance, this cartoon does not seem especially sympathetic to their plight. 1774.

This cartoon offers a hair-raising view of the Bunker Hill battle, spoofing the sort of outlandish hairdo Anna Green Winslow mentions in her diary. 1776.

Sam Webb, in a colonel's uniform in this engraving from a C. W. Peale portrait, lived through the ferocious and bloody assault on Bunker Hill, shown in this picture of the burning of Charlestown. From the *Correspondence and Journals of Samuel Blachley Webb*, edited by W. C. Ford, 1893.

A Front VIEW of YALE-COLLEGE, and the COLLEGE CHAPEL, in New Haven.

Yale College as Elijah Backus knew it did not change much through wartime, though classes were removed to Wethersfield, Connecticut, due to the threat of enemy action. From *Captain Nathan Hale* by G. D. Seymour, 1941.

This view of the Hudson River's west bank is how it looked to a British officer before "Gentleman Johnny" Burgoyne surrendered at Saratoga in the battle described by Oliver Boardman. 1777.

Tracy's horse came too. Lathrop brought it. Breed's brother has not sent a horse for him, but he has hired one here. April fools are not as plenty today as the pigeons were yesterday, for they flew over in such numbers that we may reasonably expect to be plentifully supplied with them this season.

April 2. Tracy, Breed, James, and myself set out from New Haven this morn and after various incidents, viz., stops, drams entirely composed of flip, a plentiful dinner and a large quantity of childish conversation, we arrived at Colchester where we had a warm fire, a good bowl of egg-punch, an excellent supper, a good bed to lie on, and your petitioner farther saith not.

Colchester, April 2, 7 p.m. In general Congress assembled. To all to whom these presents may come, greeting: *Whereas*, it may happen in the course of human events that mankind may be ignorant of the true causes and reasons of our delay at this place at the present time, and *Whereas*, several disaffected and evilminded persons have taken occasion from it to misrepresent and abuse us, all which is contrary to our dignity and the grandeur of our exalted station—Be it known unto you that the question was proposed: Whether we should proceed to the town of Norwich, the 2d instant or not, when after a very long and warm debate, we for several weighty and important reasons in our great wisdom concluded and resolved, *nimine contradicente*, to tarry here till the 3rd and then forward to the place above mentioned. Given under our hand, April 3, [sic] 1777. Elijah Backus, President.

April 3. Set out from Colchester about 6 o'clock and arrived at Norwich about 9, where we ate breakfast. Just as we arrived home it began to rain.

April 5. Pater [father] had orders from the government to make another cannon. I have permission to go and have the smallpox. . . .

April 7. James and I set out from Norwich this morn, the sun about an hour high, and went to Mason's and found that he was gone. We accordingly went as far as a tavern about 4 miles from Windham, towards Hampton, and while our horses were eating, Bushnell, Mason and Tiffany rid up and dismounted. When we had stayed here a sufficient time we embarked and rode as far as Pomfret and dined. At this place I saw Dr. Waterman and Beriah Bill. We again embarked and with but two more stops arrived at Uxbridge at Dr. Willard's, where not being able to get entertainment, we went to Colonel Reed's tavern and put up. I am very tired and have a great pain in my breast and left arm.

April 8. Feel something better. We have been inoculated.

April 9. Storrs came to the doctor's last night and is to live here and is inoculated.

April 11. As nothing worthy of notice happens, shall omit several days.

April 14. Walton went to hospital today. Our inoculation has all taken except Bushnell's.

April 16. Mr. Uxbridge was at the doctor's this morn. About 10 o'clock, Bushnell, Mason, James and myself set out from Dr. Willard's attended by Abraham Willard. We have Mr. Williams's horse to carry our packs and Jemmy rode on it as he was the smallest. We walked about four miles when my symptoms came on so hard that I was unable to go afoot, so James dismounted and I rode the other two miles as far as Colonel Smith's, where we left our things and proceeded to the hospital about 12 o'clock, where we were shown the hospital and its inhabitants, particularly Huntington who was the most horrible sight I ever saw. Here we found Mr. Williams, Colonel Dyer's son, and several others we were acquainted with. The melancholy, the mournful, and the deathlike aspect of the place, the dismal-looking flags that were hung in the air to keep off all comers to our habitation, attended with the sickness with which I was afflicted, made the place destined to be the receptacle for persons in my condition appear more like the infernal regions than any other place I ever had any idea of. For three days I continued sick, waiting for the appearance of the pock.

April 21. My symptoms have left me and I feel much better.

April 22. I have about two or three hundred pock and James about the same number. Walton is broken out and has thousands of pocks but he bears them with bravery and patience. Bushnell is broke out, the last of our number.

April 29. Mrs. Vedder has sent me the second part of my pies and says she has sent them all. I sent 4 quarts of apples to her and she sent back about 3 quarts of apple pies, crust and all, those poor miserable things. O Tempora! O Mores!

April 30. We have been in the hospital two weeks and have not had one clear, warm day. Benjamin and Christopher Backus and Eliphalet Huntington came to Mendon last night and were at the hospital this morn, and we are to ride their horses back. Bushnell, James and I washed up and deserted the land of the ragged visionaries. Bushnell stayed at Colonel Smith's, and we took the horses and proceeded to Dr. Willard's at Uxbridge. After several attempts an old gentleman, Colonel Spring, agreed to keep our horses till next Monday, and we went to our lodgings.

May 1. This day have I completed my eighteenth year, and what am I?—an awkward, foolish boy—conducted from infancy by an unseen hand through various dangers, seen and unseen, fed and clothed by its bounty and brought to the present time, sensible of my own littleness and inability to perform anything either to the service of my Master or greatly to the advantage of mankind.

May 3. We had news of the regulars destroying the stores [provisions] at Danbury and of the engagement our people have had with them, in which we had the misfortune to have General Wooster mortally wounded and several others killed, among whom is Dr. Atwater of New London. The regulars have retreated to their ships.

May 9. John Hillhouse was at our house and brings news that General Wooster is dead.

May 10. The old militia men go down to New London in droves in order the more handily to pursue the laudable exercise of fighting.

May 23. I carried my gun up to Weston's to have a bayonet put on it.

June 21. [At Wethersfield with Tutor Timothy Dwight.] The scholars come into town, but slow. . . .

June 23. There are 17 or 18 scholars in town and 'tis likely there will not be much over 20.

June 24. We attend exercises regularly at the schoolhouse.

June 25. I brought in a composition this evening: "If you are highly unhappy either in your person, your abilities, or your fortune, wait not for miracles to change you but conduct yourself under your present circumstances in such a manner as will be most for your own advantage.—Backus."

July 22. Our [commencement] exercises began at 3 P.M. and were not ended till about 6.

October 19. Hear that [British] General Burgoyne and his

whole army, numbering 4,500 men, are cut up and will be surrendered as prisoners of war.

December 31.
> I'm swiftly wafted down the tide of life
> And soon shall enter on the endless scenes
> Of the huge ocean of eternity
> Where never ceasing rolls the great Abyss.
> —*Backus*

—Ellen D. Larned,
"Yale Boys of the Last Century,"
Connecticut Quarterly
1 (1895): 355–61.

PRISONER OF WAR ABROAD

Charles Herbert, age 19

Mill Prison, Devon, England, 1777

*C*aptured by the British navy at sea, Charles was first held in the
sunken hull of a prison ship, and ended up in Mill Prison, in
England. Considered a traitor to Great Britain, like all Americans
he was denied prisoner-of-war status there and so subjected to brutal
treatment by staff and visitors. Food and water were rationed. Water
was so scarce few prisoners could maintain anything like sanitation;
food was often spoiled and scabby and consumed raw for lack of fire.
If blankets or clothes wore out they were not replaced. Even infested
with bugs and lice they were the only protection against the dirt-
covered floors and the damp, moldy stone walls, bitingly cold in
winter, suffocatingly humid in summer. In such crowded rooms,
prisoners died of cold, hunger, or diseases like smallpox, dysentery,
yellow fever or diarrhea which caused an unbearable stench to mingle
with that caused by overcrowding in unventilated areas and lack of

sanitation of any kind. Those prisoners caught trying to escape were placed in the "black hole," even worse for being solitary confinement. Those sent to exercise in the "itchy yard" were hardly less fortunate, for there they caught "the itch," a virulent form of scabies especially tormenting. Bonded in misery, the inmates risked such punishment to help a fellow prisoner try to escape. Most resigned themselves to enduring the misery and making the best of it.

A multitalented Yankee, Charles fared better than most. He made boxes out of scrap wood for the guards, or for sale to curiosity-seekers who came to see the prisoners. He also played shoemaker and manufactured cigars—anything to make money for extras and pass the time. At night he would secretly write in his journal, using pencils and paper scrounged during the day. As each page was finished he would secret it in his boot until finding a chance to hide it for good in the false bottom of a sample box. He was also able to buy books from the guards at inflated prices and so set up a little lending library for fellow prisoners, to help them pass the time also and to make their bestial existence more bearable.

☆   ☆   ☆

January 15. We hear that the British troops have taken "Fort Washington," with the loss of eight hundred men.

January 16. A number of seamen's wives came on board [the prison ship] today, and upon being told that they had American prisoners on board, "Have you?" said one to the other. "What sort of people are they?" "Are they white?" "Can they talk?" Upon being pointed to where some of them stood, "Why!" exclaimed they, "they look like our people, and they talk English."

March 27. We are told that we are to go on shore tomorrow to prison. Our company, one after another, are daily dropping sick, and about forty of us have the itch. But our sick have as good care taken of them on board this ship as we could expect, and we are visited morning and evening by the doctor.

March 28. I have been poorly some days past, and having no appetite for my food. I bought a quarter of a pound of sugar to sweeten some water gruel, which is the best that I can get here.

March 29. Today two more were sent on shore to the hospital, sick.

March 30. Sunday. But the time is badly spent for persons in our situation, who do not know how soon the gallows may be our doom. . . .

April 5. Last evening the master-at-arms told us that we were to go on shore today at ten o'clock, but we are not there yet. Today we had an opportunity of reading a newspaper, wherein is an account of the Americans taking 900 Hessian troops on Christmas evening. As we are not allowed a paper, when we get one we are obliged to be very cautious how and when we read it.

November 17. This day I am twenty years of age. I have often read in authors of some great transaction to be laid out to the world in the year 1777, and I have been looking for it, in hope of seeing the event. But, alas! little did I think that at the age of twenty years I should have spent almost a twelve-month of my time a prisoner.

November 18. It has been reported for several days past that Philadelphia is taken. I believe I may assert with truth, that since we have been taken, we have heard fifty times that Philadelphia was taken, and often I have seen it in the papers, and many people believe it. It is in this manner that the poor and common people in England are blinded by false reports; and some of the gentlemen of Plymouth hired the sexton to ring the bells for rejoicing.

November 30. Last evening, it being very dark and stormy, we were in general resolved to put in execution a plan proposed—to dig out at the backside of the prison, seize the sentry, confine him, and carry him out of call, but not to hurt him. Upon breaking ground, they unexpectedly saw a lamp placed near the hole, which gave light all round, so that they thought it impracticable to put their design into execution. I think if it had been otherwise, nearly two-thirds in prison would have gone out. I got myself dressed and ready and was in hopes of getting out, but to my sorrow I find myself still in Mill Prison.

December 3. This morning the guard discovered another hole which we begun to dig yesterday. I think we have been very diligent and careful to improve every opportunity to make our escape, but the guard is so strict with us that I think it almost impossible to succeed, and we have reason to think that there are traitors amongst us.

December 7. Sunday. It is a great grievance to be shut up in prison and debarred from hearing the gospel preached on the Lord's day, though I did not make much improvement of it when I had the opportunity.

December 8. Today we were all mustered and, after this was over, the agent informed us that he had received a letter from the Board to put all on half-allowance [half rations] for breaking orders and attempting to make our escape, until the transgressor should be found out. But as we all with one voice joined in one cause, we thought it inhuman to pitch upon any one man. Therefore, by way of contribution, we raised money enough to hire one man to own the same and suffer for all, so that we are obliged to support him while on half-allowance and make him amends for his sufferings.

December 9. Today the man delivered himself up to go to

the Black Hole, and the agent allows him every indulgence consistent with his orders, which is a very uncommon thing for him.

December 11. There have been various reports for several days past, but I thought them not worthy of observation because they did not come from so good authority as I could wish they might. But today we have a very authentic account from Captain Henry Johnston's brother, who is lately from London, that General Burgoyne and his army are totally routed, many killed, and taken to a man. And as I do not doubt the truth of it, it gives me more satisfaction than any news I have heard since I have been a prisoner. Also, we have good reason to believe that Howe is in possession of Philadelphia, but Washington, of choice, without any molestation, let him march in, for we hear that the Americans have possession of all the forts on the river.

December 16, 17. We have a paper wherein is a confirmation and the particulars of General Burgoyne's being taken, with six thousand men, seven thousand stand of arms, seven thousand suits of clothes, seventy thousand guineas [over two million dollars in today's currency], sixty bateaux [boats], with a thousand barrels of provisions, and a great many pieces of artillery, which in England they acknowledge to be the best ever sent out of the country against any nation. We have also a melancholy account of the cruelty of the Indians in the back settlements, set on by the inhuman Burgoyne, and an account of [American General Benjamin] Lincoln's taking two forts up North River and putting the people to the sword. We hear, besides, of General Washington's giving Howe battle and after battle was over, there were six hundred wagon loads of dead and wounded seen to go into Philadelphia. After hearing this news, joy is plainly seen in the countenance of every American here.

1778

April 26. For some months past we have thought it presumption to try to make our escape from prison by digging out, on account of there being traitors amongst us. An innocent man has borne the scandal of this a good while, but upon being told of it by a friend, he took no rest day or night until he had found the traitors, and upon examination we discovered them to be a man and a boy. Accordingly they were tied up and whipped. The boy was whipped by a boy, two dozen and a half lashes on his bare back. And we thought it the man's prerogative who had borne the blame of being a traitor and was innocent, to lay the stripes upon the man. Accordingly he gave him three dozen upon his bare back and spared not. Had the traitor stayed till night, he would have left his ears [ie:, they would have been cut off], but I suppose that he was suspicious of that, so he went and jumped over the gate and delivered himself up to the guard and told his story. The boy was sent for, so now they are both separated from us in another yard, and it is well for them that they are so.

April 27. A man came out of the Black Hole, his time being up, and Mr. Boardman and Deal, who have been only 17 days on half-allowance in the prison hospital, were sent into this yard. They are the only persons who have broke out and been taken, who have not suffered forty days on half-allowance in the Black Hole.

April 28. Last evening being somewhat dark, two young men had a mind to try to make their escape, one of whom cut his hammock and blanket into strips and tied them together, got over the wall at the end of the prison into the yard and was there caught and sent to the Black Hole. Today all the Negroes were taken out of this prison and put into a separate building called the "itchy yard."

April 29. Today is Wednesday, which is our payday, and each man received sixpence. And as we have received it regularly for some weeks past, we are told that we are to have it weekly, so in future, I shall only mention when we do not have it.

—R. Livesey, ed., *Prisoners of England*
(Boston: Rand, 1854).

WATCHING THE BRITISH SURRENDER AT SARATOGA

Oliver Boardman, age 20
Ticonderoga, New York, 1777

O liver's diary gives an eyewitness account of the turning point of America's fortunes. France and other would-be allies hesitated to help, uncertain that the Americans could beat the all-powerful British forces. Burgoyne's surrender showed them that Americans could win. Oliver, as a member of the ragtag and bobtail troops that made it happen, accepted the crucial event only for what it meant to him, namely the chance, now that the battle was over, for him to go back home. He belonged to the Connecticut militia, an arm of the state like today's national guard, only dependent upon the state for money which sometimes ran out. If he had fought for the army raised by Congress, called Continentals, at least he could have been sure of receiving land if not the $5.00 a month standard pay—$6.67 if he brought his own weapon. The army also would have supplied shirt, blanket, linen, and straw for bedding, firewood for meals plus an

65

iron pot to cook them in and a canteen for water. The trouble was that he would have been stuck for at least six months' enlistment.

Serving under General Benedict Arnold (not yet a traitor), Oliver and his buddies fought alongside the Continentals and were probably just like them statistically. Their ages ranged from 11 to 42; 42 percent were in their teens; 52 percent in their twenties. They were mostly farmers or workingmen and included African-Americans and Indians. When it was available, they all shared the same rations daily: a pound of beef or three-quarters of a pound of pork or one pound of salted fish; a pint of milk; three pints of peas or beans; a half-pint of rice or Indian meal; and one quart of spruce beer or cider. Troops in "flying camps," such as Oliver describes, were always on the move and seldom had the luxury of these rations. As he shows, these troops lived with death, either from friendly fire—as when sentries shot their own sentries in the impenetrable woods—or from enemy patrols or Tory guerillas.

They suspected the Indian allies also. Congress had spent $17,000 for rum and other gifts to keep them at least neutral. Those serving as scouts with Oliver's troops were probably Onondagas from the Iroquois Nation. The vengeance they take on the captured Tory here was not unusual for redmen or white. Painting the prisoner's face humiliated him, made him a non-person, and therefore fair game for whatever torments they could devise. The Hessian soldiers taken prisoner were treated more leniently since they were only hired guns, natives of Hesse in Germany brought over under contract to fight the rebels. Burgoyne's mistake in forcing their cavalry to walk through the dense woods was, as Oliver reports, now compounded by his plan to break his surrender agreement with American General Gates. The Hessian officers objected to this breach of honor. As the fight concludes, Oliver goes home.

☆ ☆ ☆

September 16. This morning we were paraded at three o'clock with our packs for a march, but retired. A melancholy accident happened this day. A soldier that had been sick at the hospital came into camp and ate a hearty meal of pot pie that was not well cooked and died in half an hour after. A couple of French doctors cut him open and found what he ate lay like a clod in his stomach. This I saw. Likely the means of sudden death.

September 17. At three o'clock this morning we were paraded for a march but soon retired.

September 18. This morning at three o'clock struck our tents and took our packs and the whole of General Arnold's division marched on towards the enemy by columns through the woods till our right was in full view of their camp. Our advanced party upon the left fired upon a number that was adigging potatoes, wounded some and took four or five prisoners. Then we retreated to the brow of a great hill and lay in the bushes for them. Our generals saw them paraded and march forward. We tarried awhile and then marched to camp [nine miles].

September 19. The enemy came to pay us a visit. When they arrived within a mile and a half, our men attracted them. A heavy fire began and lasted about four hours and a half. We hear the enemy have lost a great number. Besides wounded, 46 were taken prisoners.

September 20. Deserters come in who say the enemy are in as great confusion as ever militia was without commanders. . . .

September 21. This morning struck tents and paraded. General Arnold come to the head of the regiment and gave news that our men had taken some outworks at Ticonderoga with 300 prisoners, at least 100 of our own, and 300 bateaus loaded with baggage. Then we gave three cheers. After it had all gone through the camp, thirteen cannon were fired for the thirteen united states, then three cheers were given through the camp. This afternoon a scout of our Indians took a Tory. The General gave him to them for a while. They took him and buried him up to his neck and had their powow around him. After that, they had him up and laid him aside of a great fire and turned his head and feet awhile to the fire, hooting and hallowing round him. Then he was handcuffed and sent to Albany jail.

September 22. A sad accident happened yesterday of one sentry who shot another, being out of his post, belonging to the same picket.

September 23. A scout of our Indians took two regulars' sentries yesterday. After taking their hats from them, they painted their faces and brought them in. Besides, our Indians brought eight other prisoners in that were agoing express to Montreal. One of them was a deserter from our train of artillery at Quebec.

September 24. Our Indians went out and brought in three prisoners with a rope round the neck of each of them. We also hear that General Washington has had a smart action to the southward. Besides, another sad and melancholy accident happened of one sentry shooting another belonging to the same picket.

September 25. A party of our men went out to take the regulars' advanced pickets. Our men in surprise upon them demanded of them to lay down their arms, which they were about till an officer stepped up and damned them off hearty. They directly took their arms, made one fire, and took to their heels. Our men killed six and took one, Hessian officer.

October 7. This afternoon about three o'clock, [British

General John] Burgoyne's flying camp, commanded by [Brigadier General Simon] Fraser, advanced within about half a mile of our advanced picket to drive them from a hill where Captain Blague and 50 men and myself one of the number were posted, at which they kept a smart cannonade for a quarter of an hour while our men mustered along and sent a party to come upon their backs. They soon fell at it on all sides and drove the enemy back from their artillery to the Hessian camp where our General [Arnold] little thought of danger, forced his way through, and spared none till a ball broke his leg and killed his horse.

But his brave men, not discouraged with their misfortune, drove them from their camp and took it with their tents standing and pots boiling, besides three pieces of brass cannon—eight brass cannon in the whole, two twelves, the others sixes and nine-pounders taken today. Fraser was killed.

October 8. Our men kept a constant cannonade all day into their other encampment. General [Benjamin] Lincoln by a chance shot had his leg broke, I hear. General Burgoyne's aid-de-camp with a number of others were taken yesterday. Our men returned home to camp about dark.

October 9. About thirty deserters came in last night. They inform that Burgoyne began his retreat last night as soon as our men ceased firing, and left three hundred sick and wounded. We learn General Burgoyne wrote to General Gates to take care of his sick and wounded, as he would be glad to have his, suppose himself was routed and obliged to make the best of his way. A very rainy day, but few of our army followed their retreat.

October 10. This morning we paraded and marched after the enemy up at Saratoga and paraded over night upon a great hill about southeast from the enemy. General Schuyler's house with the rest of the buildings, mills, barracks, etc. at Saratoga were burned today.

October 16. A parley was beat at midnight last night. Our men answered it. By what we can learn his honor [Burgoyne] was about to fall from his agreement with General Gates [to surrender]. We also learn that he dealt out sixty rounds of cartridges to the British soldiers in order to do his best and worst once more, and ordered as many for the Hessians, but they refused to take them. Our generals are together taking the matter into consideration. Orders to strike tents immediately and everything put up.

Our generals sent in at 11 o'clock that they would give his honor one hour to consider the matter of his agreement yesterday, and gave orders for every man to be ready at the minute after 12 o'clock when three cannon will be fired if he will not sign the articles of capitulation.

Colonel Morgan received orders for his riflemen to march immediately and scale their works and spare no man they could find, and the army to follow and carry it through. Our scout took a Tory that deserted from us at Ticonderoga. Without any trial they put a rope round his neck and tied it to a saddle and told him they would hang him. He begged and prayed they would shoot him. Then they tied him to a tree and gave him a hundred lashes. Then he begged they would hang him. Now he is to receive two hundred more, which two mornings will complete, and then to be tried by a court martial for his life.

October 17. The hand of Providence worked wonderfully in favor of America this day. According to the agreement of General Burgoyne yesterday, he marched his army out of his works at ten o'clock in brigades and paraded their arms on the meadow at Saratoga. At three o'clock in the afternoon they marched through our army that was paraded on the right and left, with a guard for Boston. . . .

October 27. This afternoon I marched home.

—"Journal of Oliver Boardman of Middletown,"
Collections of the Connecticut Historical Society
7 (1899): 223–32.

Part III

☆ ☆ ☆

On the Home Fronts

1777–1781

Before the British occupied Philadelphia, Congress sped off to safety in Lancaster County to the west. Many Philadelphians remained, some because they had no other place to go, some to give aid and comfort to the occupying troops, and some because they deplored the violence on both sides and tried to see what reasoning could do to reach a compromise. From September 1777 to June of the following year, the occupation troops treated them all with varying degrees of contempt.

The British did try to encourage business as usual, since Philadelphia was the second largest city in the empire. But by bad luck, this turned out to be the coldest winter many could remember. Supplies grew scarce, tempers short, paranoia set in with shorter days. Yankees upriver sailed a few empty nail kegs down the Delaware to Philadelphia harbor. The British panicked, thinking they were boobytraps filled with gunpowder. This was one of the few laughs the common folk had that winter.

Those who remained loyal to the British, called Loyalists or Tories, enjoyed life as ever. Even on the eve of their departure the British officers mounted a ball the likes of which had never been seen on these shores. They and local belles all dressed up in Persian costume and feasted on exotic delicacies, while outside the common folk damned them to hell. When the British pulled back to New York for strategic reasons, their collaborators went with them, some unwillingly, for they sensed that the Philadelphians would expect their pound of vengeance.

Despite the best intentions of their officers, the occupying troops had acted like occupation troops everywhere at all times in history, living off the land and sparing neither friend nor foe. Many Philadelphians who at first welcomed the

British as guardians of the old law and order now had a complete change of heart as they saw their streets denuded of trees, their fields and larders depleted on demand, their wives and daughters sexually compromised.

The religious sect called Quakers, or Friends, bore the brunt of oppression. Although the colony had been founded by Quakers and descendants of William Penn still were proprietors, Quakers no longer enjoyed the political or economic power they once had. Now the pacifism which was part of their religion made them suspect. During the occupation they had carried on business as usual but would not cooperate with the British army. After the occupation, they published pamphlets urging an end to the war, and this made the returning Yankees suspicious.

Notice of a fictitious plot appeared in local newspapers and, on suspicion of subversion alone, leaders of the Quaker community were sent off to exile on the frontiers of Virginia. Their families remained to protect their homes against maurauders and the new laws that requisitioned the private property of collaborators. Only a succession of appeals by Quaker wives persuaded Congress to free their menfolk, but all remained under a cloud of suspicion.

Those families who had left the city to escape the occupation found the war enfold them even in the countryside. British raiding parties scoured the land looking for supplies and Americans dashed about trying to find the floating front lines. Private homes became headquarters for officers, their outbuildings bivouacs for troops. With their sons and brothers and lovers at the front, young women socialized with troops from the other colonies, in transit to the front lines. This was one way friendships were formed that would eventually blossom into family ties binding a new nation.

A QUAKER PACIFIST
SUFFERS

Robert Morton, age 16
Philadelphia, 1777

*R*obert's diary shows clearly how beset with conflicting loyalties or feelings civilians could be during the Revolution. As a Quaker, Robert was one of the moneyed class of Philadelphians—citizens of the second largest city in the British empire at that time—who had earned their wealth through shrewd trading. By religious conviction, Quakers were opposed to violence, and so Quaker leaders were exiled from the city to the Virginia frontier by the Yankees because they opposed the war and were suspected of being British sympathizers. Robert's stepfather was such a man, so the boy and his mother were left to fend for themselves as armies marched in and out of the city. This, too, bred its problems. Robert—whose skepticism about nearly everything but the danger of fire is clear here—was happy to see the rambunctious Yankees leave, but the British, in spite of good manners at first, soon showed their true colors. In addition, Robert's people were trapped by* *military law: when their homes were plundered by the British troops they sought redress, but being Quakers they could not condone the stiff military punishment meted out to perpetrators. On top of that, Robert watched as the homes of those exiled as British sympathizers were destroyed by the British as strongholds of Yankee resistance! Perhaps this is why his tone is so sarcastic throughout much of this excerpt.*

☆ ☆ ☆

September 19. This morning, about one o'clock, the express arrived to Congress, giving an account of the British army having got to the Swede's Ford on the other side of the Schuylkill [River], which so alarmed the gentlemen of the Congress, the military officers and other friends to the general cause of American Freedom and Independence that they decamped with the utmost precipitation and in the greatest confusion, insomuch that one of the delegates, by name Fulsom, was obliged in a very *Fulsom* manner to ride off without a saddle. Thus we have seen the men, from whom we have received and from whom we still expected protection, leave us to fall into the hands of (by their accounts) a barbarous, cruel, and unrelenting enemy.

O Philadelphia, my native city, thou that hast heretofore been so remarkable for the preservation of thy rights now sufferest those [the Quaker leaders] who were the guardians, protectors, and defenders of thy youth, and who contributed their share in raising thee to thy present state of grandeur and magnificence with a rapidity not paralleled in the world, to be dragged by a licentious mob from their near and dear connections and by the hand of lawless power banished from their country unheard, perhaps never more to return, for the sole suspicion of being enemies to that cause in which thou art now engaged; hadst thou given them even the form of a trial, then thou wouldst have been less blameable, but thou hast denied them that in a manner more tyrannical and cruel than the Inquisition of Spain.

September 25. This morning the news arrived of the British army being about 5 miles from the City. In the evening they sent a letter to Thomas Willing desiring him to inform the inhabitants to remain quietly and peaceably in their own dwellings and they should not be molested in their persons or property. [I] set up till one o'clock patrolling the streets for fear of fire. Two men were taken up who acknowledged their intentions of doing it.

September 26. About 11 A.M. Lord Cornwallis with his division of the British and auxiliary troops amounting to about 3,000 marched into this city . . . to the great relief of the inhabitants who have too long suffered the yoke of arbitrary [Yankee] power and who testified their approbation of the arrival of the troops by the loudest acclamations of joy.

September 28. About ten o'clock this morning some of the Light Dragoons stationed near our plantation broke open the house—2 desks, 1 bookcase, and 1 closet besides several drawers and other things—and ransacked them all. I applied to their officer, who informed me that if the men were found out they should be severely punished. I have been informed that a soldier this day received 400 lashes for some crime, which I do not know.

September 29. Went with Dr. Hutchinson to Israel Pemberton's plantation where we found destruction similar to that at our plantation—3 closets being broke open, 6 dozen bottles of wine taken, some silver spoons, the bedclothes taken off, 4 beds, one ripped open, the tick [mattress cover] being taken off, and other destruction about the plantation. The officers were so obliging as to plant a sentry there without application.

Upon our return home we passed through part of the camp and saw a man hanging.

September 30. This morning my mother and I went to Colonel Harcourt, commander of the Light Dragoons near our plantation, to make intercession for the men who are apprehended for breaking and ransacking our plantation and house. The Colonel upon my application behaved very unlike a gentleman by asking me what I wanted in an ungenteel manner, and told me he could not attend to what I had to say, and said that the trial was coming on and I must attend to prosecute them.

I informed him there was a lady who would be glad to speak with him. He then came to my mother and behaved in a very polite, genteel manner and assured her that he could not admit her application as the orders of the General must be obeyed, and that the soldiers were not suffered to commit such depredations upon the King's subjects with impunity. Some of the British troops came to my mother's pasture on Friday and Sunday last and took away two loads of hay without giving a receipt or offering payment.

We had a verbal account this morning of the prisoners [exiles] being seen on Wednesday last at Carlisle on their way to banishment. It is reported that the Continental troops have erected several batteries on the other side of the river to annoy and distress their enemy. One at White Hill, one at Trenton, and one nearer to the city.

October 1. The man who was found guilty of robbing our plantation received punishment this day, which was —— lashes. The man found coming out of Mary Pemberton's plantation house is sentenced to be executed. Mary Pemberton has petitioned the General for mitigation of the punishment.

October 2. The Quartermaster General of the Light Horse

took one load of hay from our pasture, which he promises to give a receipt for. For the two loads taken before by order of the Quartermaster, Second Battalion Grenadiers, he has given me a receipt for 100 pounds [of hay] which two loads Jacob declares was near 1,000 pounds. 'Tis said Lord Howe with the Fleet arrived in the River last week.

October 3. A foraging party went out last week towards Darby and brought in a great number of cattle to the great distress of the inhabitants.

November 15. We received a letter from my father by way of Wilmington giving an account of their being permitted to ride six miles from their dwellings. . . .

November 20. We this morning received a letter from my father dated at Winchester the 12th instant. He informed us that the exiles had received no intelligence from here these six weeks, and expressed an earnest solicitude for our welfare in this time of general calamity and distress. They had received no answer from Governor Henry to their remonstrance, by which they [believed] they are not to be sent further, but we imagine they have received an answer [not] conducive to their release. They had seen a Baltimore paper doubtless filled with gross misrepresentations and falsehoods respecting our situation which, added to their not hearing from us for such a length of time, must have occasioned alarming apprehensions concerning us: that on the 24th the roaring of cannon had been heard within 100 miles of the city; that he [Robert's stepfather] had written 15 letters since their arrival at Winchester, 5 only of which we have received.

November 22. This morning about 10 o'clock the British set fire to Fair Hill mansion house, Jonathan Mifflin's, and many others amounting to 11 besides outhouses, barns, etc. The reason they assign for this destruction of their friends' property is on account of the Americans firing from these houses and harassing their pickets. The generality of mankind being governed by their interests, it is reasonable to conclude that men whose property is thus wantonly destroyed . . . will soon be converted [to enemies of the British].

But what is most astonishing is their burning the furniture in some of those houses that belonged to friends of [the British] government, when it was in their power to burn them at their leisure. Here is an instance that General Washington's army cannot be accused of. There is not one instance to be produced where they [the Americans] have wantonly destroyed and burned their friends' property. But at the last action at Germantown with the same propriety as the British they could have destroyed Benjamin Chew's house and [thus] would have injured a man who is banished in consequence of his kingly attachment.

The other side has destroyed most of the houses along the lines, except William Henry's, which remains entire and untouched while J. Fox's, Dr. Moore's, and several others are hastening to ruin, so that if [the British] want to make any distinction, it is in favor of their open, professed and determined enemies.

December 14. This evening, Dr. Drewet Smith returned from Winchester, to the great amazement of his friends and fellow citizens, having been confined better than three months. He says that the Lieutenant of the county told them [the exiles] they were at liberty to go where they pleased. He, with the knowledge of his fellow-prisoners, left them on Monday last. This extraordinary and unexpected affair may occasion the remainder being more closely confined, or else have a discharge with a permission to return home. It appears that no orders have been given concerning them since the election of our new council by the Assembly.

The British army, on their last excursion to Abington and Chester County, plundered a number of the inhabitants of everything they had upon their farms and abused many old, inoffensive men. Some of them have applied for redress but have not obtained it.

December 15–20. E. E. returned this week from his journey and left Winchester and 3rd instant, came through Yorktown, and says the Quakers are to be removed to Staunton, Virginia [for conspiring to damage the value of American money, Continental currency].

—"The Diary of Robert Morton,"
Pennsylvania Magazine of History and Biography
1 (1877): 2–39.

ENTERTAINING
PASSING TROOPS

Sally Wister, age 16
Outside Philadelphia, 1777

*W*hile Robert Morton remained in occupied Philadelphia, other Quakers sent their families into the countryside for safety's sake. Sally's relatives had a large farm about fifteen miles out of town. It was on a road heavily traveled by Americans retreating before the British occupied the city and reentering after the British withdrew. She was thus in a position to meet many young officers from the different colonies, especially after General Smallwood adopted the farm as his headquarters—as Sally describes. Since he was in charge of troops from Maryland and New Jersey, she and they could easily have mutual acquaintances, always a good opening for conversation.

Like that of Becky Franks, Sally's attitude may be seen changing as she writes about her experiences. Saucy and pert to the very wealthy but shy young major from the South, she gradually sees the dangerous *life he must lead. Her own situation seems hardly less threatened, with troops of both sides hurrying along outside, drunken soldiers coming inside, reports of ruin becoming routine. Sally gets used to it. Unlike Becky Franks, she gradually shifts from playing coquette to putting up a good front for the soldiers' morale. Like countless other young girls, Sally resigns herself to never seeing her major again.*

Because her parents had been well off before the war, Sally had the best education available to girls of that era. She attended the pioneering girls' school of Quaker Anthony Benezet, who insisted that each student learn the classics at least as well as any boy. That is why Sally's journal-in-letter-form is filled with scholarly allusions. Debby Norris, the friend she pretends to be writing to, had been her classmate at Benezet's school and would easily understand the allusions and, as a Quaker, would converse as well in the plain style of speaking using "thee" instead of "you." It turned out that Debby never did read the journal until 1830, two dozen years after Sally's death.

☆   ☆   ☆

Though I have not the least shadow of an opportunity to send a letter if I do write, I will keep a sort of journal of the time that may expire before I see thee. The perusal of it may sometime hence give pleasure in a solitary hour to thee and our Sally Jones.

Yesterday, which was the 24th September, two Virginia officers called at our house and informed us that the British army had crossed the Schuylkill [River]. Presently after, another person stopped and confirmed what they had said and that General Washington and his army were near Potts-grove.

Well, thee may be sure we were sufficiently scared. However the road was very still till evening, about seven o'clock, when we heard a great noise. To the door we all went. A large number of wagons with about three hundred of the Philadelphia militia. They begged for a drink and several pushed into the house.

One of those that entered was a little tipsy and had a mind to be saucy. I then thought it time for me to retreat. So figure me, mightily scared and not having presence of mind enough to face so many of the military, running in one door and out another all in a shake with fear. But after awhile, seeing the officers appear gentlemanly and the soldiers civil, I called reason to aid, my fears were in some measure dispelled though my teeth rattled and my hands shook like an aspen leaf. They did not offer to take their quarters with us, so with many blessings and as many adieus, they marched off. I have given thee the most material occurrences of yesterday faithfully.

September 25. This day till 12 o'clock the road was mighty quiet when Hobson Jones, riding along like a madman, he made a stop and said the British were at Skippac road, that we'd soon see the light horse and a party of Hessians had actually turned into our lane. My Dadda and Mamma gave it the credit it deserved, for he does not keep strictly to the truth in all respects, but the delicate chicken-hearted Liddy [twenty-year-old friend] and we were wretchedly scared. We could say nothing but, "Oh, what shall we do! What will become of us!?!" These questions only augmented the terror we were in.

September 26. My, dear, there's nothing like courage. 'Tis what I stand in need of myself, but unfortunately have little of it in my composition.

I was standing in the kitchen about 12 when somebody came to me in a hurry screaming, "Sally, Sally, here are the light horse!" This was by far the greatest fear I had endured. Fear tacked wings to my feet. I was at the house in a moment.

At the porch I stopped, and it really was the light horse. I run immediately to the western door where the family were assembled anxiously waiting for the event.

They rode up to the door and halted, inquired if we had horses to sell. He was answered negatively. "Have not you, sir," to my father, "two black horses?" "Yes, but have no mind to dispose of them." My terror had by this time nearly subsided. The officer and men behaved perfectly civil. The first drank two glasses of wine, rode away bidding his men follow, which after adieus in number they did. The officer was Lieutenant L. Lindsay of Bland's regiment, [Major Henry] Lee's troop. They to our great joy were Americans and but four in all. What made us imagine them British— they wore blue and red, which with us is uncommon.

October 19. Now for new and uncommon scenes. As I was laying in bed and ruminating on past and present events and thinking how happy I should be if I could see you, Liddy came running into the room and said there was the greatest drumming, fifing, and rattling of wagons that ever she heard. What to make of this we were at a loss. We dressed and were downstairs in a hurry.

Our wonder ceased. The British had left Germantown and our army were marching to take possession. It was the general opinion they would evacuate the capitol. Sister Betsy, myself, and George Emlen went about a half mile from home where we could see the army pass. Thee will stare at my going, but no impropriety, in my opinion, or I would not have gone. We made no great stay but returned with excellent appetites for our breakfast.

Several officers called to get some refreshment, but none of consequence till the afternoon. Cousin Prissa and myself were sitting at the door, I in a green skirt, dark, short gown, etc. Two genteel men of the military order rode up to the door. "Your servant, ladies," etc. Asked if they could have quarters for General Smallwood. Aunt Foulke thought she could accommodate them as well as most of her neighbors, said they could. One of the officers dismounted and wrote "Smallwood's Quarters" over the door, which secured us from straggling soldiers. After this he mounted his steed and rode away.

When we were alone, dress and lips were put in order for conquest, and the hopes of adventures gave brightness to each before-passive countenance.

In the evening his Generalship come with six attendants, which composed his "family," a large guard of soldiers, a number of horses and baggage wagons. The yard and house was in confusion and glittered with military equipment. There was great running up and down stairs, so I had an opportunity of seeing and being seen, the former the most agreeable, to be sure. One person in particular attracted my notice. He appeared cross and reserved, but thee shall see how agreeably disappointed I was.

October 20. I dare say thee is impatient to know my sentiments of the officers, so while Somnus [sleep] embraces them and the house is still, take their characters according to their rank. The General is tall, portly, well made, a truly martial air, the behavior and manner of a gentleman. A good understanding and great humanity of disposition constitute the character of General Smallwood. . . . Captain Furnival I need not say more of him than that he has, excepting one or two, the handsomest face I have ever seen. A very fine person, fine light hair, and a great deal of it, adds to the beauty of his face.

Well, here comes the glory. The major, so bashful, so

famous, etc., he should come before the captain, but never mind. I at first thought the major cross and proud, but I was mistaken. He is about 19, nephew to the General, and acts as major of brigade to him. He cannot be extolled for the graces of person, but for those of the mind he may be justly celebrated. He is large in his person, manly, with an engaging countenance and address.

October 21. I just now met the Major, very reserved, nothing but, "Good morning" or "Your servant, madam." But Furnival is most agreeable. He chats every opportunity but luckily has a wife. I have heard strange things of the Major— worth a fortune of thirty thousand pounds independent of anybody. The Major moreover is vastly bashful, so much so he can hardly look at the ladies. (Excuse me, good sir, I really thought you were not clever. If 'tis bashfulness only, we will drive that away.)

October 26. A very rainy morning, so like to prove the officers in the house all day. Afternoon, the General and officers drank tea with us and stayed part of the evening. After supper, I went into aunt's where sat the General, Colonel Line, and Major Stoddard. So Liddy and me seated ourselves at the table in order to read a verse book. The Major was holding a candle for the General, who was reading a newspaper. He looked at us, turned away his eyes, looked again, put the candlestick down, up he jumped, out of the door he went.

"Well," said I to Liddy, "he will join us when he comes in." Presently he returned and seated himself on the table. "Pray, ladies, is there any songs in that book?"

"Yes, many."

"Can't you favor me with a sight of it?"

"No, Major, 'tis a borrowed book."

"Miss Sally, can't you sing?"

"No." Thee may be sure I told the truth there. Liddy, saucy girl, told him I could. He begged and I denied, for my voice is not much better than the voice of a raven. We talked and laughed for an hour. He is very clever, amiable, and polite. He has the softest voice, never pronounces the "R" at all.

November 1. Today the militia marches, and the General and officers leave us—heigh, ho, I am very sorry, for when you have been with agreeable people 'tis impossible not to feel regret when they bid you adieu, perhaps forever. When they leave us, we shall be immured in solitude. The Major looks dull. About two o'clock, the General and Major come to bid us adieu. With daddy and mammy they shook hands very friendly. To us they bowed politely. Our hearts were full. I thought Major was affected: "Goodbye, Miss Sally," spoken very low. He walked hastily and mounted his horse.

The Major turned his horse's head and rode back, dismounted. "I have forgot my pistols"—passed us and ran upstairs. He came swiftly back as if wishing through inclination to stay, by duty compelled to go. He remounted his horse. "Farewell, ladies, till I see you again"—cantered away. We looked at him till the turn in the road hid him from our sight. I wonder whether we shall ever see him again.

December 5. Oh gracious, Debby, I am all alive with fear. The English have come out to attack (as we imagine) our army. They are on Chestnut Hill, our army three miles this side. What will become of us only six miles distant? We are in hourly expectation of an engagement. I fear we shall be in the midst of it. Heaven defend us from so dreadful a sight. The Battle of Germantown and the horrors of that day are recent in my mind. It will be sufficiently dreadful if we are only in hearing of the firing to think how many of our fellow creatures are plunged into the boundless ocean of eternity, few of them prepared to meet their fate. But they are summoned before an all-merciful judge from whom they have a great deal to hope.

December 6. No firing this morn. I hope for one more quiet day. Four o'clock, I was much alarmed just now, setting in the parlor indulging melancholy reflections, when somebody burst open the door: "Sally! Here's Major Stoddard." I jumped.

Our conjectures were various concerning his coming. The poor fellow, from great fatigue and want of rest together with being exposed to the night air, had caught cold which brought on a fever. He could scarcely walk, and I went into aunt's to see him. I was surprised. Instead of the lively, alert, blooming Stoddard who was on his feet the instant we entered, he looked pale, thin, and dejected, too weak to rise or bow, and "How are you, Miss Sally?" "How does thee do, Major?"

I seated myself near him, inquired the cause of his indisposition, asked for the General, received his compliments. Not willing to fatigue him with too much chat, I told him adieu. Tonight, Aunt Hanna Foulke, senior, administered something. Jesse assisted him to his chamber. He had not lain down five minutes before he was fast asleep. Adieu. I hope we shall enjoy a good night's rest.

December 7. I tripped into aunt's. There sat the Major rather more like himself. How natural it was to see him. "Good morning, Miss Sally." "Good morrow, Major. How does thee do today?"

Major: "I feel quite recovered, Sally."

"Well, I fancy this indisposition has saved thy head this time."

Major: "No, ma'm, for if I hear firing, I shall soon be with them." That was heroic.

About eleven, I dressed myself—silk and cotton gown. It is made without an apron. I feel quite awkwardish and prefer the girlish dress.

December 8. 'Tis amazing how we get reconciled to such things. Six months ago, the bare idea of being within ten— aye, twenty—miles of a battle would almost distract me, and now, though two such large armies are within six miles of us, we can be cheerful and converse calmly of it. It verifies the old proverb that "Use is second nature."

In the afternoon, we distinctly heard firing. Everyone was at the door, I in horrors. The armies were, as we judged, engaged. Very composedly, says the Major to our servant, "Will you be kind enough to saddle my horse. I shall go." Accordingly the horse was taken from the hospitable quiet barn to plunge into the thickest ranks of war. Cruel change.

[Mr.] Seaton insisted to the Major that the armies were still nothing but skirmishing with the flanking parties. "Do not go." We (us girls, I mean) happened to be standing in the kitchen. The Major passing through in a hurry, I forsooth showed a strong "partiality" by saying, "Oh, Major, thee is not going!" He turned round, "Yes, I am, Miss Sally," bowed and went into the road.

We all pitied him. The firing decreased, and after persuasions innumerable from my father and Seaton, and the firing over, he reluctantly agreed to stay. Ill as he was, he would have gone. It showed his bravery, of which we all believe him possessed of a large share.

December 11. Our army moved to go into winter quarters, but we hear there is a party of the enemy gone over the

Schuylkill, so our army went to look at them. I observed to Stoddard, "So you are going to leave us to the English?"

"Yes, ha, ha. Leave you for the English." He has a certain indifference about him sometimes that to strangers is not very pleasing. He sometimes is silent for minutes. One of these silent fits was interrupted the other day by his clasping his hands and exclaiming aloud, "Oh, my God, I wish this war was at an end."

Noon. The Major gone to camp. I don't think we shall see him again.

—Albert C. Myers, ed.
Sally Wister's Journal
(Philadelphia: Ferris and Leach, 1902).

NEW YORK *VERSUS* PHILADELPHIA SOCIETY

Rebecca Franks, age 20
Flatbush, Long Island, N.Y., 1781

*N*o *Tory debutante was more celebrated than Becky Franks. Her dark, flashing eyes and brilliant repartée enlivened British parties when their troops occupied Philadelphia, and later in New York City when she and her father were exiled for consorting with them. New York remained in British hands throughout the war, and since the Franks had a summer place on Long Island, it was no problem for them to leave Philadelphia. The war was furthest from Becky's mind at first, but in this letter to sister Abby her anxiety breaks through. Abby understood the fashionable French phrases, the jargon about "love making" (teasing, flirting) among the redcoated British officers, and the latest fashions. But Becky makes a great point of reassuring Abby that she is not so frivolous as she used to be. She contrasts the artificiality, insincerity, and shallow behavior of New Yorkers with that of the more natural, brighter Philadelphians, really*

94

showing the difference between manners inspired by monarchy in Great Britain and those evolving with the new nation headquartered in Philadelphia and representing a fusion of cultures from the thirteen states. Becky clearly prefers Philadelphia society, but what concerns her more is the foolishness of elder brother Moses, who wants to join the American army. She is disturbed not because he wants to remain American but because she fears for his health! Even this social butterfly realizes that war can be hazardous to health, at least.

☆ ☆ ☆

August 10. You ask a description of the Miss Van Horne that was with me—Cornelia. She is in disposition as fine a girl as ever you saw—a great deal of good humor and good sense. Her person is too large for a beauty, in my opinion, and yet I am not partial to a little woman. Her complexion, eyes, and teeth are very good, and a great quantity of light brown hair: entre nous [between us], the girls of New York excel us Philadelphians in that particular and in their forms. A sweet countenance and agreeable smile. Her feet, as you desire, I'll say nothing about—they are Van Horne's and what you'd call Willings [socialite family of Philadelphia]. But her sister Kitty is the belle of the family, I think, though some give the preference to Betsy. You'll ask how many thousand [daughters] there are, only five. Kitty's form is much in the style of our admired Mrs. [Grace] Galloway, but much taller and larger—her complexion very fine, and the finest hair I ever saw. Her teeth are beginning to decay, which is the case of most NY girls after eighteen, and a great deal of elegance of manner.

By the by, few New York ladies know how to entertain company in their own houses unless they introduce the card tables except this family, who are remarkable for their good sense and ease. I don't know a woman or girl that can chat above half an hour—and that on the form of a cap, the color of a ribbon, or the set of a hoop-stay or jupon [vest].

I will do our ladies, that is, Philadelphians, the justice to say they have more cleverness in the turn of an eye than the NY girls have in their whole composition. With what ease have I seen a Chew, a Penn, Oswald, Allen, and a thousand others entertain a large circle of both sexes, and the conversation without the aid of cards not flag or seem the least strained or stupid. Here, or more properly speaking, in NY, you enter the room with a formal set curtsey and after the how do's, 'tis a fine or a bad day, and those trifling nothings are finished, all's a dead calm till the cards are introduced, when you see pleasure dancing in the eyes of all the matrons, and they seem to gain new life.

The misses, if they have a favorite swain, frequently decline playing for the pleasure of making love—for, to all appearances, 'tis the ladies and not the gentlemen that show a preference nowadays. 'Tis here, I fancy, always leap year. For my part that am used to quite another mode of behavior, I cannot help showing my surprise, perhaps they call it ignorance, when I see a lady single out her pet to lean almost in his arms at an assembly or playhouse—which I give my honor to have too often seen both in married and single—and to hear a lady confess a partiality for a man who perhaps she has not seen three times: "Well, I declare, such a gentleman is a delightful creature, and I could love him for my husband," or "I could marry such-or-such a person." And scandal says most who have been married, the advances have first come from the ladies' side, or she has got a male friend to introduce him and puff her up. 'Tis really the case, and with me they lose half their charms—and I fancy there would be more marriage was another mode adopted. But they've made the men so saucy that I sincerely believe the lowest ensign thinks 'tis but ask and have—a red coat and smart epaulette is sufficient to secure a female heart.

I was obliged to cut just as I finished the *heart*. General Robertson, Commodore Affleck and Major Murray made their appearance, and as I was writing in the parlor quite *en dishabille* [undressed], I was obliged to make the best of my way out. I am glad of it, as it broke my ill-natured train of ideas. I am quite ashamed of it. There is too much truth to have it known, but if it should be known I'll throw the blame on you, as 'twas owing to the question you asked of this family. . . . Lord! If this letter is seen I shall be killed. If it is, I must fly to you for protection. You may imagine what an indifferent I am to continue writing and beaus in the room. But so it is—I am not what I was. . . .

And now, my dear Abby, I am going to tell you a piece of news that you'll dislike as much as I do. What think you of [older brother] Moses coming out with a cockade! He writes to papa and me 'tis his serious resolve, and we must not be surprised if we see him this Summer. The idea of entering an ensign at his time of life [thirty-something] distresses more than anything I've met with since I left you. All the comfort I have is that his Uncle Moses will not allow him. I have not had an opportunity of asking Papa's opinion of it, as I received the letters since I've been here. But I am certain he must disapprove of it as much as I do. Was he ten or twelve years younger, I should not have the smallest objection—but 'tis too late for him to enter into such a life. And after the indulgence he's ever been used to, he'll never brook being commanded from post to pillar by every brat of boy who may chance to be longer in the service. Tomorrow I shall write to him and make use of every argument I am mistress of to dissuade him from so mad a project, which I hope will arrive in time to prevent it, for if he once enters, I would be the first to oppose his quitting it—as I ever loved a steady character. The danger of war I have in a measure reconciled myself to. 'Tis only his age I object to and the disagreeable idea of his being sent the Lord knows where.

Yesterday the Grenadiers had a race at the Flatlands, and in the afternoon this house swarmed with beaus and some very smart ones. How the girls would have envied me could they have peeped and seen how I was surrounded, and yet I should have felt as happy if not more to have spent the afternoon with the Thursday party at the Woodlands [Abby's estate]. I am happy to hear you're out there, as the town must be dreadful this hot summer. NY is bad enough, though I do not think 'tis as warm as Philadelphia. . . .

—"Letter of Miss Rebecca Franks,"
Pennsylvania Magazine
of History and Biography
23 (1899): 303–09.

Part IV

☆ ☆ ☆

*The Dislocations
of War*

1779–1781

After leaving Philadelphia the British made major advances along the southern front, easily taking Savannah, Georgia, and then Camden, South Carolina. As they penetrated inland, their ranks swelled with American Tories whose skill at frontier fighting more than matched the drill of the European-trained British. But their presence only added fuel to the patriots' will to fight, and when they met on King's Mountain, in frontier North Carolina in October 1780, it was the American militias from the Carolinas and Georgia who won—for they, too, were skilled in fighting from tree to tree. The British began the retreat that would end with Cornwallis's surrender at Yorktown.

Meanwhile, Washington's ranks had also been swelling with new kinds of fighters. These were officers like Pulaski and Kosciusko from Poland, Lafayette from France, and von Steuben from Germany who quickly trained the American amateurs in the skills of European warfare, including such basics as drilling and military courtesy, and particularly discipline. While looked down upon by their French allies as a bunch of amateurs, the Americans showed that they were more skilled than their European counterparts at horsemanship in the rugged American terrain. More vulnerable on the open plains, however, and most unfamiliar with the countryside outside their own colonies, the Americans had to depend on their foreign allies to help rout the more experienced British.

Just as the patriots had turned for vengeance to the Tories in Philadelphia, so did they in the South—even those who had not helped the British. The fighting was much more severe. William Pierce, adjutant to the American commander, General Nathanael Greene, saw "the people of this country cutting each others' throats, and scarce a day passes but some

102 / THE DISLOCATIONS OF WAR, 1779–81

poor deluded Tory is put to death at his door." He blamed it
on their common enemy: "The people, by copying the manners of the British, have become perfectly savage." Trooper
James P. Collins saw "parts of the human frame lying scattered
in every direction," remnants of the ferocious fighting. Four-
teen-year-old Andrew Jackson, as a cavalry scout, saw it as "a
game of hanging, shooting, and flogging." To rub in their
mutual contempt, each side would bury the enemy dead so
poorly that the remains would be unearthed by hogs. Common people, no matter how hungry, "would live on little meat
rather than eat hogs."

This was the result of Americans fighting Americans in
the backwoods, but the tide of history was flowing along the
seaboard. On his march from the South, Cornwallis burned
such major ports as Charleston. That city's losses were incal-
culable. It was the gateway to the Caribbean when the West
Indies thrived as crossroads of trade all over the world,
including the Far East. Besides the obvious economic losses,
there was a disastrous morale problem with large scale dis-
placement or death of Carolinians in the conqueror's path
along with the usual sexual and psychological abuse that
accompanied warriors.

As Cornwallis pushed North he faced punishing raids on
his supply lines along with attacks on the garrisons left to
occupy Savannah and Charleston. By the time he reached
Virginia in 1781, he was virtually cut off by the combined
forces led by Washington, which included veteran French
soldiers, double the number of Americans, plus the French
warships blocking any aid by sea. Nevertheless, at the surrender at Yorktown it was Washington who broke ground for the
ramparts and flew the American flag: there was no question

of who owned the victory. Cornwallis gave up 7,000 crack British troops, bringing the war to a virtual close.

In the celebration following the surrender, French and British officers toasted one another as professionals, ignoring the Americans. If Americans in the field felt the contempt of foreign allies, those passing through cities suffered from civilian contempt, especially after townspeople no longer feared Cornwallis's marauders. Troops from other regions found it hard to understand why people in such cities as Richmond would treat them this way, considering that soldiers were serving at great sacrifice to their own families and towns. General Washington himself was dismayed to find citizens of free Philadelphia looking at his troops with apathy or antipathy, attitudes he found prevalent in proportion as the British fell back to surrender at Yorktown. Self-interest *still* reigned in the colonies, in spite of victory.

SCOUTING ENEMY LINES ON HORSEBACK

Baylor Hill, age 17

Georgia and South Carolina, 1779

*A*s soon as he turned sixteen, Baylor joined the light horse, or cavalry. He was a Virginia boy, but rather than enlist in the local militia he chose to join Washington's combined forces and saw fighting in Pennsylvania before being sent south as described in his (previously unpublished) diary.

Most of Baylor's entries talk about the tedious, routine, often miserable duties of a cavalry scout. The excerpts here show how the American troops met opposition from their own fellow Americans as well as from the British. Some Americans, like the citizens of Williamsburg, ignored the war and tried to go on with business as usual. They gave no support to troops like Baylor's en route southward to protect them against the advancing enemy. Other Americans stayed loyal to the British, and still others were speculating investors, out to make fast money at anyone's expense.

The Yankees, hardly more than boys, came from different regions and were unfamiliar with the territory, easily a no-man's-land after dark, but just as bad in daylight when the civilians could be friend or foe. Horses could be stolen or lost or commandeered, leaving a trooper isolated in a strange land. Baylor's position was doubly bad since his commander, Count Casimir Pulaski, was from Poland and, like the French officers, could not speak English. Worse still, the foreign officers had been trained in Europe where battles were planned for military precision in contrast to the wild warfare in the American woods and swamps. Baylor describes how they would crash through the country-side aimlessly until they stumbled onto a crossroad. He even mentions bowmen, for Americans had learned that the bow and arrow was much more effective in the woods than were the flintlock or matchlock gun. While guns would hit targets maybe once in eighty-five tries, the bow would hit once in ten, was easier to carry, and faster to reload.

Badly outnumbered, Baylor's outfit changed from pursuers of bandits to being pursued by the British, and were soon captured. Later, Baylor would be freed in a prisoner exchange and was at Yorktown to witness Cornwallis's surrender.

☆　　☆　　☆

En Route to South Carolina, 1779

May 28. This morning we marched from the Court House to Mr. ———'s to breakfast, and to Williamsburg at night, where we was received by the major part of the inhabitants as indifferently as usual, as the enemy at present was clear of our coast. This night, Mr. Pemberton and self was obliged to take our rest out in the Commons, no such thing as lodging to be had for soldiers in town. Speculators and others of the same likeness had again returned to town and engrossed everything of the like kind.

About Forty Miles from Augusta, Georgia, 1779

August 14. Being joined by Colonel Twiggs with about 90 or 100 militia, they mounted on horseback, we proceeded down on our way to detect a party of robbers commanded by McGirt, which was in the neighborhood of Bryer Creek yesterday, and after stopping on our way two or three times to eat watermelons and to let our horses graze, we arrived within five miles of the party which we were in pursuit of— we were then about 40 miles from Augusta—where we halted from about 12 o'clock at night till day.

August 15. This morning at daybreak the whole of our party, consisting of about 150 men, marched. And after riding very fast for nine or ten miles, we came up with McGirt at Mr. Lockhart's on Buckhead Creek where we put them to flight, killed five, six wounded, and took six prisoners, with 23 horses, arms, etc. It was supposed McGirt's party consisted of about 25 men, the remaining eight men of the party made their escape into the creek on foot, among which was McGirt himself after a very narrow escape.

September 19. This morning 40 of our dragoons with eight officers was joined with Count Pulaski's legion and a party of light horse. [We] marched, as I expected, in pursuit of McGirt, a noted horse thief who has left Savannah a few days ago with a large quantity of horses, negroes, and cattle, etc. on his way to St. Augustine. We continued down 15 miles to Ogeechie Ferry, where he crossed. There being but one boat, it was tedious crossing. But after Pulaski's legion and a small part of Colonel Horry's had crossed, we received orders from Pulaski to procure forage and provision in that neighborhood for our party and to remain at the Ferry till his return. I with two of our officers went a mile from the Ferry to a farmer's house and got a good dinner and an excellent drink of punch, and after, returned to our regiment.

Near Savannah, Georgia, 1779

October 5. Last night I had a very bad fit of the ague and fever. In the afternoon Lieutenant Hughes and myself took a ride out on the Augusta road, where we had a fine view of Savannah at a half-mile distance, and after we satisfied our curiosity we went to an orange house where we filled our pockets and returned to our quarters.

October 6. At quarters. A very heavy cannonading last night. The battery remained silent today till near night when they fired for two hours very briskly. A flag [of truce] came from the enemy today, desiring that all the women and children in town might have leave to retire in the country in the rear of our army, which was refused.

In South Carolina, 1780

April 13. At Monck's Corner till after dinner, when I walked with Mr. Whiting down to the bridge near St. Stephen's Church, about a mile from the Corner. And at my return I was warned for [assigned to be] officer-of-the-day for each regiment. I visited the guards at twelve, found all alert. I also at three rose and had the horses bridled and the men dressed, the horses being before saddled. I again returned to the house and had not been in more than 15 minutes before the alarm pistol was fired, and we immediately got up.

And when I first got to the door, the advance guard of the

British Horse [cavalry] had passed in pursuit of our picket, who was flying before them, it being an alarm in earnest. And no likelihood of our men forming [into battle position], I went 'round to the stable which was on another road that crossed at the Corner. I found my boy here with his horses. I mounted my own horse, and he [mounted] the one I rode. I retreated on a different road from most of the other men that was mounted, though the greater part of both men and officers retreated on foot, not being able to mount their horses. By the time I had got a mile, I perceived the day breaking.

April 14. At daybreak I was amoving on the road from the Corner, where we made a halt. From here we moved up about five miles higher, where we met with Colonel Horry's men halted. We stopped at this place for an hour, when we moved up about two miles, when we stopped and breakfast. Then we went up to Martin's Tavern, where we halted and took a cold cut [of meat] and got plenty of good grog, which was a great acquisition.

By this time we had collected about 50 or 60 men and most of our officers. In the evening Colonel Hawes with a detachment of a hundred infantry, which came from Virginia with the artillery, joined us. At night we went about half a mile above the tavern, where we took our rest in the woods. No alarm this night. A number of our horses passed us today without riders.

April 15. We remained in the woods where we slept last night, till the evening, when we marched to the tavern. We made but a short stay here, when we marched about five miles back of the Camden road and halted at a widow woman's house. And, after putting out our guard, we went to the house where we had not been more than fifteen minutes when we were alarmed by two of our vedettes [scouts] firing. We paraded in the greatest haste and moved off immediately into the woods, where we went without a pilot [guide] and we had not a man with us that knew a foot of the way. We continued marching and countermarching the whole night without being able of knowing once where we were. Lieutenant Parsons put his knee out of place in the alarm, and Captain Stith, who was on picket, had his forehead much hurt by his horse running him against a fence. We remained in the woods till day.

April 16. This morning early we came into the road leading from the Corner to Nelson's Ferry. We continued up some distance, when we concluded to go to Mr. Parmer's, where we were very genteely treated with everything of the best. After breakfast most of us went to sleep, as we got none last night except as our horses walked along. We also took dinner, and soon after, we were alarmed. We paraded and moved to the woods, where we received orders to return, as the alarm was from some of Colonel Horry's men coming up. We returned to Mr. Parmer's and stayed till dusk, when we marched about two miles in the pine barrens.

We remained here about three hours, when we were again alarmed. We moved our party about a mile and halted, and remained till the morning without any more disturbance.

May 1. Early this morning marched from Mr. Leigh's, and after going about two miles we came to a large savannah, where I believe there was not less than sixty horses and was told by one of the inhabitants of that neighborhood that the greater part was wild. And seeing one which we thought would suit us, we set out several of the bowmen in pursuit of him. We chased him for near an hour when we concluded to leave him. But one of the bowmen who stayed behind the rest caught him and came up with us in an hour.

May 2. At our quarters till about two o'clock when I with several of our officers was ordered to Georgetown on court martial, which was concluded about sunset. The sentence the soldier in which the court sat on, was condemned to be hung, which was put in execution at dusk as the court sat on the field and everything being in readiness by the time the sentence was approved. His crime was repeated desertion to and from our army. We returned to our quarters after the execution.

May 6. At day this morning, a negro fellow with his sword by his side came to where we camped and [mistaking us for the British] informed Colonel White he was a man of consequence among those of his color, and if he thought him worthy a captain's commission he would raise a company. And he was well acquainted with the swamp which his master was secreted, being a great rebel, and he would be the first man who would go and kill him. For his kind offer, he was ordered fifty lashes and after was half hung, cut down, and left in that situation.

We marched about 12 or 14 miles down to a certain Mr. Ball's where we came upon a captain and fourteen men of the British. We took them without hurting one. They surrendered with little or no opposition—only one pistol fired. I commanded the advance and was the preventative of many of them being put to the sword. From here the prisoners was under my care. We marched up to Leno's Ferry, where we were ordered to feed our horses. Here I was relieved as officer-of-the-day.

Captain [John] Baylor succeeded me, and about half an hour later, he was ordered to cross the river with the prisoners. There being but one boat ready when an alarm pistol was fired, and in an instant we see the approach of the British

Horse in full speed. Every man took his own way, they coming on us so suddenly and our horses being afeeding. But few of [our] Horse made their escape on horseback.

I being disappointed in my horse being moved from the place I left him, I endeavored to bridle a horse standing just by. But the noise of horses straining, hallowing of their men, and firing, it was impossible to bridle him. And being ordered by one of their soldiers to surrender, I thought it time to endeavor to make my escape on foot.

I set out across the fields and fences and after getting about 200 yards from the house, I was overtaken by one of their soldiers. He attempted several times to kill me [with his sword] but missed his stroke. I only received a small cut on the back of my shoulder and had my clothes cut in two other places. The soldier by whom I was taken took my sword, belt, and watch. My horse and accoutrements was taken about four miles off.

Thirty prisoners taken, four or five wounded, and the number killed I have never heard. All privates except myself and W. C. Medici, who acted pro tem as brigade major. From here we were conducted to Lord Cornwallis's quarters near Hughes Bridge, where we stayed that night without guard, giving parole.

—Huntington Library manuscript BR 53.

ONE JUMP AHEAD
OF THE ENEMY

Betsy Ambler, age 16
On the Road in Virginia, 1781

*T*he good times at Williamsburg that Baylor Hill had seen being
enjoyed by civilians did not last long. Betsy's diary, in the form
of a letter to her friend Mildred Smith, describes her excitement at
moving there when Virginia's government transferred from Richmond
for safety. Her father was treasurer of the new state's government and
therefore a prime target for British raiders. When the British ap-
proached from the Carolinas, he hastily took to the road with his
invalid wife and daughters Molly, age 15, and Betsy.

Betsy's diary describes how they moved from refuge to refuge, her
father sleeping in the carriage by night, subject to every rumor that
the British were coming—some of which proved true. One fact was
especially poignant. It told of a raiding party under notorious Colonel
Tarleton pursuing the new state's governor, Thomas Jefferson. Jefferson, as the biggest target of all, had early sent his family off to safety

and then took to the hills to hide with the official papers. That action would return to haunt him in his political life as an act of cowardice. But as Betsy shows, discretion is the better part of valor. She and her family survived to live happily ever after, with sister Molly, herself an invalid like her mother, marrying our eminent chief justice John Marshall in one of history's idyllic lifelong love affairs.

Richmond, 1781. My dear Mildred, our removal from York to this place, which I considered one of the calamities of my life, lost much of its bitterness when I found that you and your much loved family would also be obliged to follow, but even here we find no seat for the sole of our feet.

Another alarm this morning, should it be confirmed, is that the British are really coming up the James River.

My poor dear mother will not continue a moment! What sufferings are hers!

Friday evening. At the moment I was writing to you we had too certain confirmation that the British had landed and were actually on their way to town. Not a moment to be lost and we were off in a twinkling. My father seemed to think we hadn't a moment to lose—such terror and confusion you have no idea of—governor, council, everybody scampering. Here we shall remain with our friends, but my father will return to reconnoiter.

What an alarming crisis this is! War in itself however distant is indeed terrible, but when brought to our very doors, when those we most love are personally engaged in it, when our friends and our neighbors are exposed to its ravages, when we know assuredly that without sacrificing many dear to us as our own lives, our country must remain subject to Britain's tyranny, the reflection is overwhelming.

Louisa Court House, Tuesday. Oh, my dearest girl, I tremble
for your safety. Where were you hid when the enemy passed
your door? We only had time to learn that they were on the
road from Richmond when we were again in the carriage, and
in a few hours reached this place where it would seem
impossible for us to be in any danger.

My much loved father is full of anxiety for us. Much have
we to apprehend for him. The public office which he holds
makes it absolutely necessary for him to run no risks of falling
into the hands of the enemy. We therefore see him safely
lodged in the old coach every night, with faithful old Sam as
his guard, while we endeavor to make ourselves as comfortable
as we can in the overseer's tiny dwelling, which will scarcely
hold us all.

Thursday morning. When or where shall we find rest? Such
a journey as we have again had, and now are precisely in the
same spot we set out from!

No sooner had we committed our dear father to his
solitary confinement on the night I last wrote you and were
endeavoring to console ourselves with the idea that the miserable little hovel we were in was too solitary a situation for us
to fear any danger than, while enjoying our frugal supper of
bonny clabber [chowder], honey, etc., a terrible clatter of
horses at the door set us all scampering. The British! Nothing
but the word *British* did we hear. Upon opening the door,
however, we soon discovered a parcel of miserable militia
belonging to the neighborhood.

They had called to give notice that the enemy were
actually proceeding on their way through the country, but not
one of them could say which route they had taken. A consul-
tation of our party was then held, and if we had had one
particle of our natural reason about us, we should have quietly

stayed where we were, but flight had so long been the word that it was determined unanimously that we should be off in a moment. The nearer the mountains the greater the safety, was the conclusion. So on we traveled through byways and brambles until we could get to the main road leading to Charlottesville.

Our design was first to reach a plantation in the neighborhood of the Springs, where we were at least sure of house room and a bed (a friend of ours having removed his furniture to this place). We proceeded. We arrived just as the sun appeared in all his glory. With difficulty we got admittance— no soul being in the house—and were just spreading our pallets to rest our weary heads when the landlord, out of breath, reached the house saying that Tarleton and his men had just passed and would catch the Governor [Thomas Jefferson] before he could reach Charlottesville.

What a panic for us all! Our best beloved father had pursued the same route only a half hour before, Charlottesville being the place appointed for public officers to repair to. Fortunately, however, the enemy had got ahead of him by another road, which he by good luck hearing, he immediately joined us and hurried us back to the selfsame spot we had left the night before. Thus were we one whole night and the greater part of the next day accomplishing what placed us precisely in the same situation we were in before, a spot that I defy the British or even the devil himself to find.

Great cause have we for thankfulness, and however dreary it is I will endeavor to be contented, hoping and trusting for a speedy deliverance. But how dreadful the idea of any enemy passing through such a country as ours, committing enormities that fill the mind with horror and returning exultingly without meeting one impediment to discourage them!

It seems that they might just as easily have crossed the Blue Ridge [Mountains] as they have the Southwest Mountains. Oh! my friend, when will there be an end to our sorrows!

—"Cornwallis in Virginia,"
Virginia Magazine of History and Biography
38 (1930): 167–69;
"An Old Virginia Correspondence,"
Atlantic Monthly
84 (1899): 535–45.

AT THE
YORKTOWN SURRENDER

Ebenezer Denny, age 19
Near Yorktown, Virginia, 1781

In the final critical engagement of the war, Denny and his infantry buddies, fatigued by years of fighting through wilderness, now had to assume the formal behavior of Europeanized troops. They were assigned to American units led by the French Marquis de Lafayette and drilled by the imported Prussian general Baron von Steuben as though preparing for what today would be a media event. Denny and his comrades had been fighting under General "Mad" Anthony Wayne, called "Mad" for his impetuous bayonet charges, which contrasted starkly with the orderly disciplined tactics of the Europeans.

Now, with Washington as figurehead, the combined Franco-American force engaged the British in a long, wearying siege, wearing down Cornwallis until he surrendered as Denny describes. Denny reports how Baron von Steuben took the standard from him—a pretty good sign of the low esteem the Europeans had for these Yankee foot soldiers. Denny's outfit had slogged through swamp and forest on forced marches, wearing white papers in their hats in order to see each other at night, carrying the heavy spear-and-battle-axe combinations called espontoons only to rendezvous with the better dressed, better drilled troops from the eastern shore. Exhausted, covered with lice, and smelling like hogs, they drilled for days, only to take no part in the ceremonies anyway. Reading between the lines, we see Denny almost relieved to be marching northward again, away from the spit and polish of the Europeans and Europeanized army.

☆   ☆   ☆

June 18. Joined the troops under command of Lafayette. The Marquis had marched two or three days to meet us. His men look as if they were fit for business. They are chiefly all light infantry, dressed in frocks and overalls of linen. One day spent in washing and refreshing—in fixing arms, carriages etc., and served out ammunition. Move toward Richmond, where Lord Cornwallis with the British army lay. Heard that his lordship was employed burning and destroying warehouses of tobacco, all the public storehouses, etc.

Passed through Richmond toward Williamsburg after the enemy, joined by Baron Steuben with some new levies. Near Bacon's Bridge the British turned upon us. Our advance pressed them too close.

The army was formed for a fight—they did not come on. General Wayne very anxious to do something. Colonel Simcoe, who commands the British legion (horse and mounted infantry), is constantly committing some depredation abroad and foraging for their army. Wayne hears of him—our brigade leave their tents and baggage, march at dark, with piece of white paper in each man's hat—flints taken out.

At daylight reach place called the Bowling Green, where

Simcoe had been the evening before. This was a severe march for me—found myself asleep more than once on the route. Returned and met the baggage. A detachment from the brigade put under command of Colonel Richard Butler. After a variety of marching and countermarching, Butler at length intercepts Simcoe. A smart skirmish takes place. Wayne supports Butler, and Simcoe retreats. Here for the first time saw wounded men; feelings not very agreeable. Endeavor to conquer this disposition or weakness; the sight sickened me.

This little engagement within six miles of Williamsburg, where the enemy were encamped. Pennsylvania troops retreat—advance again. See the Marquis' light troops but seldom—know they are not far off. Kept constantly on the move. Hear that the enemy have decamped and preparing to cross James river at Jamestown. Our brigade move down; lay on arms all night about nine miles from the enemy.

At daylight move on; middle of the afternoon of the Sixth of July firing ahead. Our advance drove in the enemy's pickets, marching at this time by companies in open order. My captain (Montgomery) fell behind his company where my place was— talked with me, gives me a lesson useful to me. When perhaps within 150 yards of the enemy, we closed column and displayed; advanced in battalion until the firing commenced, and ran along the whole line.

A regiment or more of the light infantry and three pieces of artillery were in the line. Saw the British light infantry distinctly, advancing at arm's-length distance and their second line in close order, with shouldered musket, just in front of their camp—their infantry only engaged. The main body were discovered filing off to the right and left when orders were given us to retreat.

My captain, Montgomery, received a shot in his foot and

hopped back in the rear. Lieutenant Bluer being absent, the charge of the company devolved on me. Young and inexperienced, exhausted with hunger and fatigue, had like to have disgraced myself—had eat nothing all day but a few blackberries—was faint and with difficulty kept my place. Once or twice was about to throw away my arms (a very heavy espontoon). The company were almost all old soldiers. Kept compact and close to our leading company and continued running until out of reach of the fire. The enemy advanced no farther than to the ground we left.

We could not have been engaged longer than about three or four minutes but at the distance of sixty yards only. Our loss is said to be upward of one hundred killed and wounded—among the latter twelve officers, one of whom, Lieutenant Herbert, taken prisoner. A few of the wounded not able to get off were also taken. The artillery horses all killed; two pieces were lost.

Retreated two miles to very commanding ground, where we met the Marquis with our main body. Halted and had some Indian meal served out, the wounded dressed, etc. and before day, changed our ground and encamped about five miles from the field.

July 7. An officer, surgeon, and a few men, sent with a flag, to bury the dead, etc. This was done in company with an equal number of the enemy. Our wounded who were prisoners had been properly treated. The British moved from Jamestown. . . .

September 1. Army encamped on the bank of James river—part of French fleet, with troops on board, in view. Recrossed James river and encamped at Williamsburg. Army in high spirits—reinforcements coming on.

September 14. General Washington arrived. Our brigade

was paraded to receive him. He rode along the line—quarters in Williamsburg.

September 15. Officers all pay their respects to the Commander-in-chief; go in a body. Those who are not personally known, their names given by General Hand and General Wayne. He stands in the door, takes every man by the hand. The officers all pass in, receiving his salute and shake. This is the first time I had seen the General.

We have an elegant encampment close to town, behind William and Mary College. This building occupied as an hospital. Williamsburg a very handsome place, not so populous as Richmond but situate on evenly, pretty ground; streets and lots spacious—does not appear to be a place of much business, rather the residence of gentlemen of fortune. Formerly it was the seat of government and Dunmore's late residence. A neat public building, called the capitol, fronts the principal street. Upon the first floor is a handsome marble statue of William Pitt.

The presence of so many general officers and the arrival of new corps seem to give additional life to everything. Discipline the order of the day. In all directions troops seen exercising and manoeuvering. Baron Steuben our great military oracle. The guards attend the grand parade at an early hour, where the Baron is always found waiting with one or two aids on horseback. These men are exercised and put through various evolutions and military experiments for two hours—many officers and spectators present; excellent school, this.

At length the duty of the parade comes on. The guards are told off. Officers take their posts, wheel by platoons to the right; fine corps of music detailed for this duty, which strikes up. The whole march off, saluting the Baron and field officer of the day as they pass. Pennsylvania brigade almost all old soldiers and well disciplined when compared with those of Maryland and Virginia. But the troops from the eastward far superior to either.

September 25. Joined by the last of the troops from the eastward. French encamped a few miles on the right, busy in getting cannon and military stores from on board the vessels.

September 28. The whole army moved in three divisions toward the enemy, who were strongly posted at York, about twelve miles distant. Their pickets and light troops retire. We encamped about three miles off—change ground and take a position within one mile of York. Rising ground (covered with tall handsome pines) called Pigeon Hill separates us from a view of the town. Enemy keep possession of Pigeon Hill.

Strong covering parties (whole regiments) moved from camp as soon as dark and lay all night upon their arms between us and the enemy. Our regiment when on this duty were under cover and secured from the shot by Pigeon Hill. Now and then a heavy shot from the enemy's works reached our camp. Our patrols and those of the British met occasionally in the dark. A few shots were exchanged—would generally retire. . . .

October 9. The scene viewed from the camp now was grand, particularly after dark—a number of shells from the works of both parties passing high in the air, and descending in a curve, each with a long train of fire, exhibited a brilliant spectacle. Troops in three divisions manned the lines alternately. We were two nights in camp and one in the lines, relieved about ten o'clock.

October 11. Second parallel thrown up within three hundred yards of the main works of the enemy, new batteries erected, and additional number of cannon brought forward—

some 24-pounders and heavy mortars and howitzers. A tremendous fire now opened from all the new works, French and American. The heavy cannon directed against the embrasures and guns of the enemy. Their pieces were soon silenced, broke, and dismantled. Shells from behind their works still kept up.

Two redoubts, advanced of their lines and within rifle shot of our second parallel, much in the way. These forts or redoubts were well secured by a ditch and picket, sufficiently high parapet, and within were divisions made by rows of casks ranged upon end and filled with earth and sand—a deep narrow ditch communicating with their main lines.

October 14. On the night of the Fourteenth, shortly after dark, these redoubts were taken by storm; the one on the right by the Marquis with part of his light infantry—the other, more to our left but partly opposite the center of the British lines, by the French. Our batteries had kept a constant fire upon the redoubts through the day. Belonged this evening to a command detailed for the purpose of supporting the Marquis. The night was dark and favorable. Our batteries had ceased. There appeared to be a dead calm. We followed the infantry and halted about half way, kept a few minutes in suspense, when we were ordered to advance.

The business was soon over. Not a gun was fired by the assailants. The bayonet only was used. Ten or twelve of the infantry were killed. French had to contend with a post of more force—their loss was considerable. Colonel Hamilton led the Marquis' advance. The British sentries hailed them— no answer made. They also hailed the French, "Who comes there?" Were answered, "French grenadiers."

October 15. Heavy fire from our batteries all day. A shell from one of the French mortars set fire to a British frigate.

She burnt to the water's edge and blew up—made the earth shake. Shot and shell raked the town in every direction. Bomb-proofs the only place of safety.

October 16. Just before day the enemy made a sortie, spiked the guns in two batteries and retired. Our troops in the parallel scarcely knew of their approach until they were off— the thing was done silently and in an instant. The batteries stood in advance of the lines and none within but artillery. This day, the Sixteenth, our division manned the lines—firing continued without intermission. Pretty strong detachments posted in each battery over night.

October 17. In the morning, before relief came, had the pleasure of seeing a drummer mount the enemy's parapet and beat a parley, and immediately an officer, holding up a white handkerchief, made his appearance outside their works. The drummer accompanied him, beating. Our batteries ceased. An officer from our lines ran and met the other and tied the handkerchief over his eyes. The drummer went back, and the British officer conducted to a house in rear of our lines. Firing ceased totally.

October 18. Several flags pass and repass now even without the drum. Had we not seen the drummer in his red coat when he first mounted, he might have beat away till doomsday. The constant firing was too much for the sound of a single drum. But when the firing ceased, I thought I never heard a drum equal to it—the most delightful music to us all.

October 19. Our division man the lines again. All is quiet. Articles of capitulation signed. Detachments of French and Americans take possession of British forts. Major Hamilton commanded a battalion which took possession of a fort immediately opposite our right and on the bank of the York river. I carried the standard of our regiment on this occasion. On entering the fort, Baron Steuben, who accompanied us, took the standard from me and planted it himself.

The British army parade and march out with their colors [flags] furled. Drums beat as if they did not care how. Grounded their arms and returned to town. Much confusion and riot among the British through the day. Many of the soldiers were intoxicated. Several attempts in course of the night to break open stores. An American sentinel killed by a British soldier with a bayonet. Our patrols kept busy.

Glad to be relieved from this disagreeable station. Negroes lie about, sick and dying in every stage of smallpox. Never was in so filthy a place—some handsome houses, but prodigiously shattered. Vast heaps of shot and shells lying about in every quarter, which came from our works. The shells did not burst, as was expected.

Returns of British soldiers: prisoners, 6000; seamen about 1000. Lord Cornwallis excused himself from marching out with the troops; they were conducted by General O'Hara. Our loss said to be about 300; that of the enemy said not more than 550. Fine supply of [British] stores and merchandise had; articles suitable for clothing were taken for the use of the army. A portion furnished each officer to the amount of sixty dollars.

October 20. Joined by a new raised regiment from Pennsylvania. Officers hastened to partake of the siege but were too late. British troops march into the interior—to Winchester and other places. Visit Gloucester, small village opposite York; nothing seen there. Some of our officers return to Pennsylvania, others take their place. Visit Williamsburg in company with young gentlemen of the country, on horseback. Spend a few days very agreeably. Militia employed leveling the lines. Our brigade prepares for a long march.

—*Military Journal of Major Ebenezer Denny*
(Philadelphia: Historical Society of
Pennsylvania, 1859), 35–45.

Part V
☆ ☆ ☆
Forging a New Society

1781–1785

The end of fighting brought an end to the war but not to troubles, most of them deriving from the old notions of colonial self-interest. The thirteen colonies were now thirteen sovereign states each with its own constitution, legislature, and concerns. Held in loose association by the Articles of Confederation they did send representatives to Congress but without giving them power to do much more than debate. Perhaps the only important actions had to do with western lands, culminating in the celebrated Northwest Ordinance of 1787, governing territory which is now the Midwestern states. Otherwise, Congress remained more of a debating society than a national legislature, without power or appropriations to implement policy.

Nevertheless, Congress had been a thorn in George Washington's side throughout the war, since he felt morally obligated to obtain congressional authorization for conducting the war and depended on appropriations to compensate the troops. Towards the close of the war they threatened mutiny unless Congress paid them, but Washington cooled the heat by appealing to, of all things, their patriotism as Americans. In retiring from his command, he wrote to all the states' governors urging them with religious fervor to put aside self-interest for national interest. Nobody listened.

For another decade, the loose confederation proved more wobbly year by year. Finally, when farmers in western Massachusetts outraged at foreclosures attacked the courts and marched on the arsenal at Watertown, people realized the need for a central authority with clout. And more, when they saw that interstate competition in trade and commerce could ruin them and open the way for foreign governments to move back in, then the states agreed to at least convene a meeting at

Philadelphia to talk about revising the Articles of Confederation.

Until that time, however, each state minded its own business. The exceptions were important. Virginia and Maryland, for example, ceded western lands that could be used to settle debts accumulated during the war, including soldiers' pay. So compensated, many veterans started settling in the Ohio Valley or sold their bounty land to speculators who then peddled the property to Europeans, thereby generating a whole new movement of immigrants westward.

In the older settled regions, however, people tried to reconstruct the lives they had known before the war. In view of the internal struggles between British-leaning Loyalists and patriots, the old days could never come again. The Loyalists were sent into exile, their properties confiscated. Some family representatives stayed to protect what property they could, willing to suffer loss of civil rights and persecution for the sake of future generations.

Further, intermarriage among soldiers and women of different regions meant tighter networking, so that current and future generations moved more freely from region to region with consequent intermixing of cultures. The sons of financier Robert Morris, as examples, moved to upper New York State while his daughter married a Virginian. So many congressmen were marrying New York heiresses that some wag sent a letter to the newspapers urging a moratorium for the sake of local bachelors.

A third factor breaking down the separation between states came about when children were sent abroad to continue education interrupted by the war. The Morris boys mentioned above had been educated abroad. So were Jefferson's two daughters and Ben Franklin's grandson. Also in Europe were children of diplomats, like the son and daughter of John Adams. All had been born in America and grew more conscious of *being* American as Europeans distinguished them not by state or region but by nationality.

They also became more nationalistic as they contrasted the artificial manners of Europeans with the natural affability of the Americans they met abroad and remembered from home. When these expatriates returned to America, they brought back some European customs, fashions, and manners; but more important to the future, they also brought back a new sense of community that was national in scope.

It remained, then, for the Constitutional Convention of 1787 to institutionalize that spirit. State self-interest died hard. Small states fearful of their borders debated against large states jealous of their prerogatives. They hit an impasse in mid-summer before taking a break to cool off, still thinking of themselves as individual states. By the end of September, however, the draft of the Constitution which in July had started, "We the people of the states of New Hampshire," etc., now had a new beginning: "We the people of the United States. . . ."

QUAKERS UNDER SIEGE

Anne Rawle, age 19
Philadelphia, 1781

*T*he surrender at Yorktown did not bring peace to Philadelphia's
Quaker community, especially those who had served the British
during their occupation. Anne's stepfather and mother had been sent
into exile at New York, while she and sister Peggy remained behind
with relatives. Anne's letters to her mother had to be sent secretly for
fear the sisters would also be arrested, but they managed to correspond
quite regularly, providing such reports as the rioting when news of
Cornwallis's surrender sparked a city-wide celebration that went on
for days. Anyone who did not put a candle in the window was
considered un-American and fair game for busted windows or worse.
The radicals, lumped together by Anne as Whigs (vs. Loyalists or
Tories), would not forget the aid and comfort Quakers had given the
enemy and now showed a proper resentment by way of reminder.
Anne's family, descendants of Philadelphia's original settlers, were

treated harsher than most because her stepfather had been the magistrate for the British during their occupation. The other Quakers she notes as suffering damage were all of the highest class. The Mrs. Grace Galloway she mentions had owned much of Bucks County, Pennsylvania, but since her husband had been chief of police under the British, she stood to lose everything and now lived in a friend's home on charity.

☆ ☆ ☆

October 22. The first thing I heard this morning was that Lord Cornwallis had surrendered to the French and Americans—intelligence as surprising as vexatious. People who are so stupidly regardless of their own interests are undeserving of compassion, but one cannot help lamenting that the fate of so many worthy persons should be connected with the failure or success of the British army.

Uncle [Joshua] Howell came in soon after breakfast and, though he is neither Whig nor Tory, looked as if he had sat up all night. He was glad to see all here so cheerful, he said. When he was gone, Ben Shoemaker arrived. He was told it as he came along and was astonished. However, as there is no letter from Washington, we flatter ourselves that it is not true.

October 24. I feel in a most unsettled humor. I can neither read, work or give my attention one moment to anything. It is too true that Cornwallis is taken. Tilghman is just arrived with despatches from Washington which confirm it.

October 25. I suppose, dear Mammy, thee would not have imagined this house to be illuminated last night [celebrating Cornwallis's defeat], but it was. A mob surrounded it, broke the shutters and the glass of the windows, and were coming in, none but forlorn women here. We for a time listened for their attacks in fear and trembling till, finding them grow more loud and violent, not knowing what to do, we ran into the yard. Warm Whigs on one side and Hartleys on the other (who were treated even worse than we) rendered it impossible for us to escape that way.

We had not been there many minutes before we were drove back by the sight of two men climbing the fence. We thought the mob were coming in through there, but it proved to be Coburn and Bob Shewell, who called to us not to be frightened and fixed lights up at the windows, which pacified the mob, and after three huzzas they moved off. A number of men came in afterwards to see us. French and J. B. nailed boards up at the broken panes, or it would not have been safe to have gone to bed. Coburn and Shewell were really very kind. Had it not been for them I really believe the house would have been pulled down.

Even firm Uncle [William] Fisher was obliged to submit to have his windows illuminated, for they had pickaxes and iron bars with which they had done considerable injury to his house and would soon have demolished it had not some of the Hodges and other people got in back and acted as they pleased. All Uncle's sons were out but Sammy, and if they had been at home it was in vain to oppose them.

In short, it was the most alarming scene I ever remember. For two hours we had the disagreeable noise of stones banging about, glass crashing, and the tumultuous voices of a large body of men, as they were a long time at the different houses in the neighborhood. At last they were victorious, and it was one general illumination throughout the town.

As we had not the pleasure of seeing any of the gentlemen in the house, nor the furniture cut up and goods stolen, nor been beat, nor pistols pointed at our breasts, we may count our sufferings slight compared to many others. Mr. Gibbs was obliged to make his escape over a fence and, while his wife was endeavoring to shield him from the rage of one of the men, she received a violent bruise in the breast and a blow in the face which made her nose bleed.

Ben Shoemaker was here this morning. Though exceedingly threatened he says he came off with the loss of four panes of glass. Some Whig friends put candles in the windows which made his peace with the mob and they retired. John Drinker has lost half the goods out of his shop and been beat by them. In short, the sufferings of those they pleased to style Tories would fill a volume and shake the credulity of those who were not here on that memorable appearance, which ought to cover the Whigs with eternal confusion.

A neighbor of ours had the effrontery to tell Mrs. [Grace] Galloway that he was sorry for her furniture but not for her windows—a ridiculous distinction that many of them make. J. Head has nothing left whole in his parlor. Uncle [Edward] Pennington lost a good deal of window glass. Aunt [Beulah] Burge preserved hers through the care of some of her neighbors. The Drinkers and Walns make heavy complaints of the Carolinians in their neighborhood. Waln's pickles were thrown about the streets and barrels of sugar stolen.

Grandmammy was the most composed of anybody here. Was I not sure, my dearest Mother, that you would have very exaggerated accounts of this affair from others, and would probably be uneasy for the fate of our friends, I would be entirely silent about it. But as you will hear it from some one or another, not mentioning it will seem as if we had suffered exceedingly, and I hope I may depend on the safety of this opportunity. People did nothing today but condole and enquire into each others' honorable losses.

October 26. Neighbor Waln and Ben Shoemaker were here

this afternoon. Juliet [Sally Burge], Polly Foulke, and James Fisher came to see us in the evening—the conversation as usual on the late disturbances. It seems universally agreed that Philadelphia will no longer be that happy asylum for the Quakers that it once was. Those joyful days when all was prosperity and peace are gone, never to return, and perhaps it is as necessary for our society [The Society of Friends] to ask for terms as it was for Cornwallis. Juliet says all Uncle Pennington's fine pictures are broken. His parlor was full of men, but it was nothing, he said, to Nancy's illness, who was for an hour or two out of her senses and terrified them exceedingly.

—William Brooke Rawle,
"Laurel Hill and Some Colonial Dames
Who Once Lived There,"
Pennsylvania Magazine of History and Biography
35 (1911): 385–414.

THE DANGERS OF
IMPETUOUS MARRIAGE

Nancy Shippen, age 17
Philadelphia, 1783

*N*ancy's *journal reads like a romance novel. She herself read so many of them that she acts the part of romantic heroine and gives romantic names to everyone except baby Peggy. Nancy had been spoiled silly by her parents. At fifteen she had her own elegant home next door to theirs. Nor did they stand in her way when she chose to marry not the poor but dashing Frenchman, Louis Otto (called "Leander" here) but the demonic, sullen American colonel, Harry Livingston ("Lord B."), undoubtedly because he looked and acted like the hero in gothic novels—at first. Fortunately, his mother was not the typical storybook mother-in-law. Seeing her son insanely jealous and abusive to Nancy, she offered to give baby Peggy a safe home, knowing her son would not risk his enormous inheritance by harming her under his mother's roof.*

In the episode excerpted here, Nancy sacrifices her own happiness

*for the baby's future safety and security, knowing that Mrs. Living-
ston will give Peggy a fortune all her own. Nancy turns down her
estranged husband's offer of divorce in return for baby Peggy (and
Peggy's fortune), surrendering forevermore a chance at happiness with
suitor Louis. Nancy remains an estranged wife in Philadelphia, seeing
baby Peggy but seldom, yet living independently and thus disproving
the theory she alludes to in Madame de Maintenon's book that women
were born to be sex slaves and servants of men.*

☆   ☆   ☆

April 10. After breakfast rode out with Lord Worthy
[romantic name for her father]. Had a conversation about
Lord B. [her estranged husband] and dear Leander [her former
lover]. His sentiments corresponding with mine made me
extremely happy. Would to God it was a happiness that would
last. But the die is cast and my life must be miserable! Lord
Worthy sees the consequences of my unhappy choice too late.
It is well for me he sees it at all.

April 11. Saw Leander. Spoke to him. He praised my
sweet child. Good man!

April 18. This day I spent entirely alone, enjoying my
own meditations. They were not unpleasant. I feel calm and
composed and please myself with the reflection of having
conformed to the will of my parents in the most important
action of my life. O! may I reap the benefit of it! I'm sure I
shall! I have the sweetest child that ever was born. In her I
shall be most blessed.

April 21. Lady Worthy [her mother] spent great part of
the morning in my chamber with me, directing and advising
me about bringing up my sweet child. I need it much, for
sure I am a very young and inexperienced mother.

May 3. Spent a most delightful evening at Mrs. Powell's. I heard in the morning there was to be a very large company. I spent great part of the day in making preparation. I wished to look well. Set off about six o'clock. My glass [mirror] told me I looked well, was dressed in pink with a gauze petticoat, an elegant French hat on with five white plumes nodding different ways, a bouquet of natural flowers, and a white satin muff. Found a roomfull, and in the midst of them *Leander*. He told me what I believed, that I looked like an angel. Shall I confess that I felt pleased to be approved of by him? Why? Because he is my sincere friend, and was once—O! happy time!—my lover. I passed a most agreeable evening, though a large company, which is seldom the case. A most admirable supper, excellent wine, an elegant dessert of preserved fruits and everybody in spirits and good humor. It is now late and I am sleepy. Found my child well.

May 10. Miserable all day in consequence of a letter from Lord B. He tells me—O what is it bad that he does not tell me! But what affects me most is his accusing me of infidelity. Wretched, unhappy man, nothing but your being jealous and treating me ill in consequence of that jealousy should have tempted me to leave you. And now you say I left you because I loved another. Had you not deceived me by so often swearing you loved me to distraction, I should not have been the wretch I am. O, I'm wretched indeed! And the father too of my sweet baby—I'm almost distracted.

May 13. This morning I read Madame de Maintenon's advice.

May 15. I cannot agree with her that Women are only born to suffer and to obey. That men are generally tyrannical I will own, but such as know how to be happy willingly give up the harsh title of master for the more tender and endearing one of friend. Equality is the soul of friendship. Marriage, to give delight, must join *two minds*, not devote a slave to the will of an imperious lord.

May 16. Papa told me this morning at breakfast that I must send my darling child to its Grandmama Livingston. I told him I could not bear the idea of it, that I had sooner part with my life almost than my child. He told me it was for the future interest of my baby, that its fortune depended on the old lady's pleasure in that particular, begged me to think of it, and to be reconciled to it. If I know my own heart I never can. When will my misfortunes end! I placed my happiness in her! She is my all, and I must part with her! Cruel, cruel fate.

May 17. I have been so unhappy all day that I have not stirred out of my room except to dinner. Mamma then asked me if I had thought of Mrs. Livingston's proposal. I told her I had thought of nothing else. She asked my determination. I told her I would not part with my child if I could possibly help it. She then told me that Papa had determined that the child should go at any rate, that he could not be answerable for the child's losing her fortune which she would certainly do if I kept her from her grandmother. I cried all the time she was speaking and retired to my room, which I have not left since. I feel pleased, however, that I have a month to determine in and be with my angel child. I have kissed her a thousand times since, and find I love her as well as myself. I must think of something in order to keep her with me and yet secure her fortune.

May 22. I spend so much of my time in caressing and playing with Peggy that I almost forget I have anything else to do. I forget to read—to write—to work—in short I neglect the business of the day. At night I sit down and unfold my thoughts on paper. I love it much. Methinks it is almost as

pleasing as telling them to a friend. My child sleeps. I am
sitting close by her. I feel happy at present because I put off
the future prospect from my thoughts. I hope for the best and
enjoy the present moment.

May 27. I never was more happy. I kept my lovely child
with me all the time. The dear angel was the life of the
company [at her friend's tea]. Leander went past the window
while we were at tea. He looked in, and his eyes told me he
would be happy to join us, but I did not ask him. Prudence
forbid it. Why should it? He is my friend and I am his, but
because he was once my lover I must not see him. Cruel
custom. I have read or heard, I forget which, "that the best
friendship is the child of love." Why am I not at liberty to
indulge that friendship? Why? Because it would displease my
husband. . . .

June 1. My baby, thank God, is much recovered. These
six days past she has been so ill her life has been despaired of.
I nursed her attentively. I never left her more than an hour
altogether. O! what I have suffered! For several hours I
thought she was dying. What I felt then is impossible to
describe. I have been too ill myself with fatigue and want of
sleep. Mamma was much affected and fain would have taken
part of the trouble off my hands, but I would not permit it,
she being in a very weak state of health.

June 8. Called upon Emilia and took [baby] with me. We
had a very pleasant ride. I mentioned Peggy's illness. She
advised me to try the country air for the reestablishment of
the child's health. Mrs. Livingston's proposal then popped
into my head. I told her of it. She at first lamented with me,
that there should have been a necessity for my parting with
[Peggy]. Asked me if I had resolved. I told her I had—that if
[Peggy] did go—I would carry [her] myself. Emilia agreed

with me that it was best for me to go with it, said the child's ill health, the length of the journey, everything required it. And further, she said maybe after I got there, Lord B. might relent, and we might live happily together *once more*. She thought the sooner I set off the better. I agreed with her.

June 9. Nothing talked of but the journey. It is a very long one—two hundred miles—but if it was as far again, I would go to have the satisfaction of accompanying my darling child. O, I'm wrapped up in her! and if at last I should be so happy as to have it in my power to remain with her, to find that she makes an impression on the heart of her father, that he will love her, O it will be a happy jaunt for me indeed! What a sweet little mediator! Can he but relent when he sees her, his picture in miniature, will he not be glad to see me, fold me in his arms, and repent that he has treated me ill, wonder at my forgiveness and condescension, and become a new man. Happy prospect. I will immediately write to him, tell him that I am going to take our dear child to his mother's, tell him I will expect to see him before I arrive, ask him to meet us and conduct us to his mother's.

July 7. I have so much to say I do not know where to begin. I will go back to the day I set off from Philadelphia. Mamma came early, found me in tears, tried to console me. I hid my face in my mother's bosom. She cried as much as me. Papa was obliged to part us, or I should not have remembered that I had yet to put on my riding habit. O! how I felt! The idea that I was going to leave such kind, indulgent parents *perhaps forever* made me almost inconsolable. I am called to dinner—

About twelve o'clock we set off—Cleander, Kitty and Peggy, and poor me. Mamma and Maria rode a little way with us, and Papa and my brother on horseback. At last we parted.

Such a parting! I shall never forget it. I hung round the neck
of my mother, sobbing with her. Maria cried too, sweet girl,
and Peggy was almost eaten up between them.

"My dear girl," said Mamma, "return to us if you don't
find your husband altered for the better. Don't let your love
for our sweet baby tempt you to throw yourself into misery."

"No, my dear Mamma," cried I, "I will return if I don't
find *him* very much changed for the better. But the sight of
the child must make him relent, and he will treat me well for
her sake."

My dear Papa too said, "My dear Nancy, I love you very
much. Your happiness I am concerned for. Be sure you return
if you don't see a greater prospect of happiness than you ever
saw before with him."

I should write a volume if I was to write all that passed on
that occasion. I'll let it suffice to say that everything that is
tender and affectionate was said to me, and I was loaded with
presents. I cried without ceasing all the way we went that day.
I wrote to my dear Mamma from the first three stages [stops
en route]. I afterwards had no opportunity. My dear Peggy
missed her poor Grandmamma and would stroke me on the
face and say, "Poor Ma, poor Ma," although she is but one
year and seven months old.

[On the fifth night] reached Poughkeepsie. I was then
within 20 miles of Lord B., and 30 of Mrs. Livingston. I had
not heard one word from Lord B. I began to be alarmed.
After Cleander had retired to his room and the child gone to
sleep and Kitty was eating her supper in the next room, I sent
for the landlady to stay with me till Kitty returned. I asked
her if she knew any of Lord B.'s family? She said yes, that
she knew several of them, said there was *one* in particular that
was much spoke of. My heart told me who that was. She said

he was a very bad [man] and had nearly killed one of his servants very lately, and that he had a *wife and child* in Philadelphia. "Ah!" says I, "you see his wife and child before you." The woman looked petrified and I'm sure felt so.

August 8. I sent the letter [to her estranged husband] yesterday morning and in the evening received an answer— but such a one! I am ashamed to transcribe it. O! my heart! what I suffer! And must I part with you, my angel child? Yes, I must. How shall I bear it? And tomorrow is the day. O no! I can't go so soon.

August 21. [Returned to Philadelphia alone.] I have been in such a state of misery since I left my beloved child I have not been able to continue my journal. Alas! how shall I paint my sufferings at and since that dreadful moment that I parted with my beloved baby! I will not, I cannot attempt it. I will only say that I have never known a happy moment since. O! what a sacrifice! But it was for her, therefore let me try to be resigned.

August 23. My journal will now be very insipid indeed. I spend my time mostly in my room. I read when I can, but it is seldom I can collect my thoughts sufficiently. I work at my needle. I have time enough now!

December 6. Spent this morning as usual—read and worked—and drank tea in the afternoon at Mrs. Lenox's. Heard the most delightful news. My Peggy is safely arrived at New York. General Washington told Papa he saw her and kissed her, happy man! I saw Leander this evening at Mrs. Shippens'. He has been to New York and saw Peggy and kissed her, he says, a thousand times and says she looks beautiful. I am delighted beyond measure. I am sure I shall not sleep a wink tonight.

1784

March 5. O! I am so happy. I have received a letter concerning my darling child from my mother-in-law. My baby has been ill but is recovered and bids her grandmother tell me she is a good girl. Sweet baby, when shall I see you. . . .

April 10. Busily employed all day packing up for my jaunt to New York. I expect to go on Monday. How happy I feel in the thought of clasping my beloved child once more in my fond arms and pressing her to my bosom. But alas! I shall be obliged to part with her again in a few days after I have seen her, as I can't leave my [sick] mamma longer and my father won't permit me to take [the baby] from her good grandmother. Indeed prudence forbids it also, as upon her must my dear child depend. O! may I be enabled to bear all my trials with patience and fortitude.

—Ethel Armes, ed.
Nancy Shippen, Her Journal Book
(Philadelphia: Lippincott, 1935), 138–85.

PASSAGE TO
THE OLD WORLD

Martha Jefferson, age 15

Paris, 1785

*W*hen her mother lay dying, her father vowed never to marry
again and to raise their three girls as a single parent. Martha,
as the eldest, sought to console her father: "He kept his room for three
weeks, and I was never a moment from his side." In spirit if not in
fact, she was seldom far from Thomas Jefferson's side for the rest of his
life.

When Jefferson went to Paris as a diplomat to join Benjamin
Franklin and John Adams in concluding the treaty to end the war,
Martha came too. Tall, slender, and redheaded, she took after him in
appearance but was sharply observant and loved to tease her more
sober father. In this excerpt from a letter to friends back home, she
describes their voyage to Europe—which took three months—and the
astonishing way an American dignitary traveled: the crossing of the
English Channel found them both crammed into a coffinlike cabin,

only to be cheated by baggage carriers on the French side. Americans seemed like bumpkins to the French, and in Paris Martha had to undergo a makeover simply to be seen in society; she refused to have her hair crimped in the French style but consented to the corseting of the time. Despite his feelings about religion, Jefferson placed his daughter in a local convent school where Martha traded in her gladrags for a simple uniform, learned French from the boarders (the pensioners), and accompanied or stood in for Jefferson in the round of society dinners required of diplomats abroad—as is clear in the excerpt by Nabby Adams which follows this one.

☆   ☆   ☆

I am very happy in the convent and with reason, for there wants nothing but the presence of my friends of America to render my situation worthy to be envied by the happiest—I do not say kings for, far from it, they are often more unfortunate than the poorer of their subjects. I have seen the king and the queen, but at too great a distance to judge if they are like their pictures in Philadelphia. We had a lovely passage in a beautiful new ship that had made one passage before. There were only six passengers, all of whom papa knew, and a fine sunshine all the way, with a sea which was calm as a river.

We landed in England, where we made a very short stay. The day we left it, we got off at six o'clock in the evening, and arrived in France at eleven the next morning. I cannot say that this voyage was as agreeable as the first, though it was much shorter. It rained violently and the sea was exceedingly rough all the time, and I was almost as sick as the first time, when I was sick two days.

The cabin was not more than three feet wide and about four long. There was no other furniture than an old bench, which was fast to the wall. The door by which we came in at was so little that one was obliged to enter on all fours. There were two little doors on the side of the cabin, the way to our beds, which were composed of two boxes and a couple of blankets, without either bed or mattress, so that I was obliged to sleep in my clothes. There being no window in the cabin, we were obliged to stay in the dark for fear of rain coming in if we opened the door.

I fear we should have fared as badly at our arrival, for papa spoke very little French and I not a word, if an Irish gentleman, an entire stranger to us, who seeing our embarrassment, had not been so good as to conduct us to a house and was of great service to us. It is amazing to see how they cheat strangers. It cost papa as much to have the baggage brought from the shore to the house, which was about half a square, as the bringing it from Philadelphia to Boston.

From there we should have had a very delightful voyage to Paris, for Havre de Grace is built at the mouth of the Seine, and we follow the river all the way through the most beautiful country I ever saw in my life—it is a perfect garden—if the singularity of our carriage, a phaeton, had not attracted the attention of all we met. And whenever we stopped, we were surrounded by the beggars. One day I counted no less than nine where we stopped to change horses.

I wish you could have been with us when we arrived. I am sure you would have laughed, for we were obliged to send immediately for the staymaker, the mantua-maker, the milliner, and even a shoemaker, before I could go out. I have never had the *friseur* [hair stylist] but once. But I soon got rid of him and turned down my hair in spite of all they could say, and I defer it now as much as possible, for I think it always too soon to suffer.

I have seen two nuns take the veil. I'll tell you about that when I come to see you. I was placed in a convent at my arrival, and I leave you to judge of my situation. I did not speak a word of French, and not one here knew English but a little girl of two years old that could hardly speak French. There are about fifty or sixty *pensioners* in the house, so that speaking as much as I could with them I learnt the language very soon. At present I am charmed with my situation.

There come in some new pensioners every day. The *classe* is four rooms, exceedingly large, for the pensioners to sleep in, and there is a fifth and sixth, one for them to stay in the day, and the other in which they take their lessons in. We wear the uniform, which is crimson, made like a frock, laced behind, with the tail, like a *robe de cour*, hooked on, muslin cuffs and tuckers. The masters are all very good, except that for the drawing.

—Sarah N. Randolph,
"Mrs. Thomas Mann Randolph,"
Worthy Women of Our First Century,
ed. by Sarah Wister and Agnes Irwin
(Philadelphia: Lippincott, 1877): 14–15.

OBSERVING EUROPEANS

Abigail Adams (Jr.), age 17
Paris, 1784–85

*N*ot *to be confused with her famous mother, she was known as
Nabby Adams. In fact, she did not particularly like her mother
and missed her diplomat father so much that they finally let her join
him in Paris. Shy, retiring, Nabby was called "glacial" by her cousin,
yet her secret diary shows a young lady of deep feeling and passionate
prejudices. It also shows Martha Jefferson through the eyes of a slightly
older girl. Years alone do not explain the difference in observational
powers. Nabby notes revealing details about the persons and places she
visits, often with a cynical tone and a sly touch of humor.*

*Her brother John Quincy went home to Harvard in April 1784
leaving Nabby with the job of secretary to their father, future
president John Adams, now singlehandedly in charge of carrying on
American diplomacy overseas. His two colleagues, Franklin and
Jefferson, were both bedridden from various ailments during much of*

the season covered in the diary. This meant that young Nabby had to go with her father as a kind of communicator with the invalids, keeping them in touch with what was happening. Since they were surrounded by spies from England and France, she had to be circumspect about writing such material down in her diary, noting, however, the names of persons they met at the various parties she describes.

The problem was that the Americans had gone behind the backs of their French allies in making peace with England, so the French could not trust Adams. Neither could the British because of his role as instigator of hostilities.

What Nabby could not have foreseen was the split between Americans at home into pro-French and pro-British parties, her father's Federalists and Jefferson's pro-French Republicans, the beginning of the two-party political system which endures to this day. Her comments are thus clustered around the social world abroad. She objects to the way women are treated in France, even the way parents would arrange marriages for children based on money rather than love, yet she prefers French freedom to the artifice of the English. More, she prefers the natural manners of transient Americans like John Paul Jones, to such Frenchified Americans as William Temple Franklin, himself secretary to a famous family member, his grandfather Ben Franklin.

☆ ☆ ☆

August 8. We have taken a house at Auteuil, near Paris, very large and very inconvenient—about fifty little apartments, so small, most of them, as to be inconvenient for lodging. There is a large room to receive company in, and a dining room. All the bedrooms are above stairs. There is a spacious garden.

August 15. This day, by invitation, we dined with Mr.

[American consul Thomas] Barclay, in a friendly way, without form or ceremony. Mr. Jefferson and daughter dined with us, and two gentlemen who were not to be known. The dinner was in the French style. There is no such thing here as preserving our taste in anything. We must all sacrifice to custom and fashion. I will not believe it possible to do otherwise, for my papa, with his firmness and resolution, is a perfect convert to the mode in everything, at least of dress and appearance. Mrs. B. is a fine woman. The more I see of her, the greater is my approbation of her. She has a firm hold of my heart from her kindness and attention to my father, when he was sick of the fever last fall. I shall ever feel a grateful rememberance of her goodness.

August 24. Went in the morning with my papa and mamma to pay our respects to Dr. Franklin, this man on whom the world have passed such high encomiums and perhaps justly. He is now near 80 years old and looks in good health.

September 1. Dined at Dr. Franklin's by invitation—a number of gentlemen and Madame Helvetius, a French lady 60 years of age. Odious indeed do our sex appear when divested of those ornaments with which modesty and delicacy adorn them.

October 14. Mr. Jefferson sent us cards yesterday to admit us to see the ceremony of taking the veil in the convent where his daughter is to receive her education. . . . When the priest in his sermon invited all the others who were present to follow the example of these nuns, I observed the English girl who held the candle for one of them look very sharp upon the other English girl, whose countenance expressed that she knew better than all this—that she had no intention. Quite right she.

The relations of the two victims appeared less affected

than anyone present. It is very probable they are the victims of pride or wickedness. Thus these two girls are destined to pass their lives within the walls of this convent. They are not so strict as formerly. Miss Jefferson told me they were very cheerful and agreeable. They seemed to take great pleasure in contributing to the happiness of the pensioners. There were three princesses who are here for their education and were distinguished from the others by a blue ribbon over the shoulder.

This is considered the best and most genteel convent in Paris. Most of the English who send their children here for their education put them into this convent.

1785

January 7. Mr. Blanchard and Dr. Jeffries ascended at Dover [England] in a balloon and in two hours descended a league from Calais [France], to the great joy and admiration of everyone who saw them. The people of Calais received the aerial travellers with every mark of attention, respect, and admiration. They presented Mr. Blanchard with a gold box, the figure of his balloon on the cover, and presented him with letters giving him the title of citizen of Calais. They offered the same to Dr. J. but he, being a stranger, declined them, probably thinking his situation in England would be rendered more disagreeable and create jealousies by such a distinction. They likewise requested of Mr. Blanchard his balloon to put into the Cathedral Church at Calais, as the ship of Columbus was put into a church in Spain. These gentlemen have arrived at Paris. This voyage has been long projected. Their success has been quite equal to their expectations; there being but little wind, they did not make so quick a voyage as someothers have done. Mr. B. is a Frenchman, Dr. J. an American.

January 27. A small company to dine today—the Abbé Arneau; Mr. Dash, a Swedish gentleman; Colonel Humphreys, and Mr. Jefferson. Miss J. we expected, but the news of the death of one of Mr. J.'s children in America, prevented. Mr. J. is a man of great sensibility and parental affection. His wife died when this child was born, and he was almost in a confirmed state of melancholy; confined himself from the world and even from his friends for a long time. And this news has greatly affected him and his daughter. She is a sweet girl, delicacy and sensibility are read in every feature, and her manners are in unison with all that is amiable and lovely. She is very young.

Mr. S.[Smart, Jefferson's secretary] grows very sociable and pleasant. He appears a well bred man, without the least formality or affectation of any kind. He converses with ease and says many good things. He wants to go to a convent to learn French. The abbé, upon my inquiring today after Mademoiselle Lucille, told me she had gone to a convent, and added that the manners of the women of this country were so dissipated and the example they set their daughters was so bad that they were obliged to put them into convents to keep them out of this influence.

This may be generally true, but the abbé has a most detestable idea of the women of this country, perhaps justly. But I do not see how they can be otherwise—the manner of education and, above all, the shocking manner in which they are sacrificed in the most sacred of all connections [marriage], oftentimes nothing but inconstancy and wickedness can result from it.

January 30. This eve Monsieur [the] Marquis de la Fayette

called upon us for the first time since he arrived. I had neglected to be properly dressed today and was punished by not having it in my power to see him. He gave my papa and mamma agreeable accounts of our State [Massachusetts], and of Boston in particular. He says it is the best regulated and he observed the most harmony and agreement in the people of any of the states. He had visited all.

February 7. Today we dined with Mr. Jefferson. He invited us to come and see all Paris, which was to be seen in the streets today and many masks, it being the last day but one of the carnival, and to go to the mask ball in the evening, which we did not attend. I had but little curiosity to go. The description of those who have seen it has not given me spirit enough to spend all the night to be perhaps not gratified. The ball begins at one o'clock in the morning and lasts until six. There are no characters [celebrity masks] supported [carried] at them here, as in England, nor are there any variety in the dresses. Mrs. B. says it is the only amusement that is not superior here to what they have in London. She is so delighted with Paris that, she says, she shall never go to America with her own consent. Miss Jefferson dined with us—no other company.

February 14. Today we have dined with Dr. Franklin. There was a large company: our family, the Marquis de la Fayette and lady; Lord Mount Morris, an Irish volunteer; Dr. Jeffries; Mr. [John] Paul Jones. The Doctor's family consists of himself; Mrs. Hewson, an English lady; Mr. Franklin; Mr. Beach [Benny Bache] his grandson; Mr. Williams [his nephew] who is generally there. Mr. Jefferson has not been out to dine this long time. The Marquis de la Fayette I never saw before. He appears a little reserved and very modest.

Lord Mount Morris attracted my attention. He is a very

handsome man, a fine person, and an agreeable countenance. He looked inquiring, but Madame B., who is well acquainted with his lordship, engrossed all his attention. There was another Irish gentleman who was passable. Dr. Jeffries, the man of the day, I happened to be seated next at table. I made some inquiries respecting his late aerial voyage. He did not seem fond of speaking of it. He said he felt no difference from his height in the air but that the air was finer and obliged them to breathe oftener, and that it was very cold. He has been so cavilled at in the papers that I don't wonder at his reluctance at conversing upon the subject.

We had a sumptuous dinner. It is now Lent, and all the French are doomed to fish. Our French servants have purchased themselves dispensations for eating meat, because they live with us. However improbable this may appear, it is a fact if they speak the truth.

Madame the Marquise de la Fayette was quite sociable with papa, and professed to be a physiognomist. She would not allow that I was *triste* [sad], but grave.

February 21. Dined at the Marquis de la Fayette's with a circle of Americans. It was intended as a compliment, but I had rather it had been thought so to introduce us to French company. The fondness that Madame la Marquise discovers for her children is very amiable, and the more remarkable in a country where the least trait of such a disposition is scarce known. She seems to adore them and to live but in them. She has two that were presented to us. They both speak English and sing it. The Marquis appeared very fond of them likewise. He is apparently a man of great modesty and delicacy of manners.

Speaking of Mrs. [John] Jay, on whom every person who knew her when here bestows many encomiums, Madame de la Fayette said she was well acquainted with and very fond of Mrs. Jay. She added, Mrs. Jay and she thought alike. It was Mrs. Jay's sentiment that pleasure might be found abroad, but happiness could only be found at home, in the society of one's family and friends. She told my papa that Mrs. Jay did not like the French ladies—"Neither do I," said she. From the account she had heard of the American ladies, she believed she should be pleased with them, and should the Marquis ever again visit America, she would accompany him.

I was seated at table, between Mr. B[ingham] and the Irish gentleman whose name I have forgotten. He was very civil, but nothing very remarkable in him. Mr. B. was insupportably disagreeable. Mrs. B. was, as ever, engaging. To avoid singularity and the observation of the company she goes into, she wears more rouge than is advantageous to her. I was pleased with a little upon her, but she has become quite a French woman in this respect. We came home without going to the play.

February 26. Today Dr. Franklin, Mr. Williams, and a Monsieur St. Olympia, a French West Indian, dined with us. The latter has been writing upon the trade of the Americans with the West Indies. Papa breakfasted with him on Thursday. He brought a book of politics for papa to look at, and inquired if the ladies in America talked politics. Papa told him they conversed much upon politics, and that the liberties of a country depended upon the ladies. . . .

March 20. When I dined at Dr. Franklin's last Thursday, I asked Mr. [William Temple] Franklin by whom I was seated at table whether the image in the center of it represented any particular device, as I observed a crown of laurel and some figures. He said he "believed it was Love and Hymen, an old fashioned idea. You know," said he, "they used to talk of such things in former times, but at present they know better." I told him I was surprised to find it at his table. I believed it was not of his choice. He is strongly attached to the French. He told me he preferred an English lady who had acquired the graces of French manners, which, he added, were to be gained nowhere but at Paris. There is a something not to be defined that the French women possess which, when it ornaments and adorns an English lady, forms something irresistibly charming.

March 25. We went to take tea at Dr. Franklin's with Mrs. Hewson, and passed an hour very agreeably. Mr. Franklin is always sociable and is very satirical in general. The Dr. is always silent unless he has some diverting story to tell, of which he has a great collection. Mr. F. copies him in this way, and although he tells a story well, yet I do not think it a pleasing trait in the character of a young man—it appears better in age; it seems then expressive of a desire to be agreeable—which in old age is not always attended to. The Dr. has something so venerable in his appearance that he inspires one with respect. I never saw an old man more so.

May 9. Mr. [Paul] Randall and myself had a learned dissertation upon blushing, which arose from a girl passing by the carriage with a veil on, which are very common in the streets here, made of lawn, silk, or gauze and worn instead of a hat or bonnet. The latter is a thing I never have seen in France. Mr. R. observed that the blush of innocence was a better veil. I said there were few of those known in Paris. He inquired if they had any word in the French language expressive of innocence. There is not any other word but innocence, and it is almost without a use here. I said it was a very painful sensation [blushing]—I thought it a great advantage to be exempt from it. He was not of this opinion.

Mr. [James] Jarvis who had been in the shop, came to the door of the carriage. Mr. R. told him of our conversation, upon which commenced the dissertation. Mr. J. decided, not agreeably to my opinion or belief, that we never blushed but from the consciousness of something wrong in what was said or done that caused the blush. I do not believe it. A person so subject to blush as myself should be interested in removing every idea of evil from it.

When we had finished our business we went to Mr. Jefferson's, where I saw Miss J., a most amiable girl. Mr. J. has not dined out these four or five months, partly from choice. If he could discriminate, he would sometimes favor us with his company.

London

June 1. Today my father went with Lord Carmarthen to the Palace, [and] found many gentlemen known to him before. Lord C. introduced him to his majesty George III. Papa made his speech when he presented his letter [as America's ambassador]. His majesty was affected and said, "Sir, your words have been so proper upon this occasion that I cannot but say I am gratified that you are the man chosen to be the Minister."

September 2. About twelve o'clock Mrs. [Thomas] Smith from Clapham and Miss [Elizabeth Brand] called upon us. Mamma was just dressing, so I had to appear. Miss B. began to question me as to which country I liked best, France or England? I would not give a preference. "But you undoubtedly prefer England to America?"

"I must confess, Miss, that I do not at present."

Was it possible! I acknowledged the excellencies of this country. There was more to please and gratify the senses. But

I had formed such friendships and attachments in America as would ever render it dear to me. "But surely the culture is carried to a much greater degree of perfection here than in America."

"Granted."

"And you must," said Miss B. very pertly, "find a great difference between America and this country?"

"In what, pray, Miss?" said I.

"Why, in the general appearance, in the people, their manners, customs, behavior, and in everything."

"Indeed," said I, "I do not. There is so great a similarity in the manners of the people, in the two countries, that I should take them for one. If anything, I find a greater degree of politeness and civility in America than in the people of this country. And the lower class of people in America are infinitely superior to the lower class of people here."

Their astonishment was great. Was it possible I could think so! Surely the distressing war had been an impediment to all improvement and education.

—Caroline de Windt, ed.
Journal and Correspondence of Miss Adams
(New York: Wiley and Putnam, 1841), 14–80.

CAUGHT UP
IN THE NEW SCIENCE

Benjamin Bache, age 16
Passy, France, 1784–85

*B*enny *helped his grandfather most by staying out of his way.
Benjamin Franklin had taken ten-year-old Benny abroad with
him in 1776 to avoid interrupting the youngster's education. Benny
went to school in Geneva, Switzerland, and there he stayed until
rioting broke out a few years later and for safety's sake he was brought
to his grandfather's villa in Passy, a suburb of Paris.*

*Here the house was busy with secret negotiations leading to the
peace treaty with England. The place was filled with both French and
English spies trying to fathom Franklin's next move, while he played
the part of a garrulous old man interested only in wine, food, and
young women. Even his colleagues John Adams and John Jay were
never entirely sure what Franklin was up to, so it is not surprising
that young Benny never mentions the momentous events taking place
all around him. In spite of the fact that his grandfather was America's*

first world-class scientist, Benny seems hard put to distinguish between the absurdity of mesmerizing trees, and genuine first experiments in manned space flight, by balloon. He displays an American enthusiasm for both. Remarkably, his diary is free of the social observations that filled the diaries of Nabby Adams and Martha Jefferson, doubtless because his grandfather did not indulge him socially.

☆   ☆   ☆

January 15. An aerostatic globe one hundred feet in diameter has been constructed at Lyons. It is to start today. If the wind should be southeast, it would come; but it blows very hard from the southwest

January 28. At last the aerostatic balloon has started from Lyons with seven men, but it fell soon afterwards and very near the place of its departure.

March 2. I have been to the Champs de Mars to an experiment in which a person named Blanchard was to direct the aerostatic globes, and take a natural philosopher with him; but many accidents having happened upon the spot, he was compelled to ascend without the wings by means of which he was to guide himself, and without the natural philosopher who was to perform the experiments, so that this was nothing but a repetition of what Mr. Charles performed at the Tuileries on the first of December 1783. He came down in an hour very near the starting place.

May 22. Mr. Delon, who possesses the animal magnetism, has asked the French Academy to examine his secret. The Academy has named several persons for that purpose, among others my grandpapa, at whose house the commissioners are assembled today with Mr. Delon who, after having magnetized [hypnotized] many sick persons, they are gone into the garden to magnetize some trees. I have been present at it; it thus occurred:

Mr. Delon has made many passes towards a tree with a cane, then they brought a young man with his eyes bandaged whom Mr. Delon had brought with him (and whom he had cured of a paralysis which extended over half his body, by means' of animal magnetism, in the space of three weeks). They made him embrace several trees for two minutes. At the first three trees he held in this way, he said that he felt a numbness which redoubled at each tree. Finally, at the fourth, he remained by the tree and no longer answered. Then he fell, and they carried him upon the turf, where he made many singular contortions; then he suddenly arose.

June 23. Today, at three quarters after four, there started from Versailles an enormous balloon filled with air rarified by heat and carrying Mr. Pilatre de Rozier and another person named Prouts. It came down at half after six between Champlatreux and Chantilly. Thus it travelled twelve leagues in three-quarters of an hour. I saw it pass over Passy at five o'clock and disappear at ten minutes after five. It was hidden in a cloud, and they met with snow, which reached the earth in rain.

July 11. The Abbé Miolan and Mr. Jarmuet have constructed an aerostatic balloon more than one hundred feet high by eighty-four feet, or thereabouts, in horizontal diameter, and they have advertised it with much emphasis as certain of its success and have made a subscription, according to which the subscribers are to be present at four trials of the means of guiding it and then to make experiments upon the air at a very great height.

The first trial was fixed for today at the garden of the Luxembourg at twelve precisely. The balloon was to carry four men. As it was by means of air rarified by fire, the balloon took fire and the trial did not succeed. The King of Sweden and many other persons of consideration waited until three o'clock, and the infuriated people rushed upon the balloon and tore it to pieces. Everyone carried off some samples of it, some of the pieces large enough to make quilts, and I believe that the authors would have experienced the same fate if they had not been escorted by a detachment of the French Guards. They have not yet given any account to the public of the money which they received.

July 13. I rose very early, as likewise all the family, to go see a balloon which the Duke of Chartres has caused to be constructed. It is enormous, in the form of a cylinder terminated by two hemispheres. It is to be filled with inflammable air. We have, therefore, been to Saint Cloud, where we believed that it was to start, but it has been postponed to another day.

In the evening I went to Saint Cloud with Alexandre to learn for certain when it would start. I inquired of a gentleman of my acquaintance who was at this time guarding the balloon. He told me it would be Thursday.

July 15. I went again to Saint Cloud to see the balloon start. It was in the shape of a cylinder, terminated by two hemispheres thirty feet in diameter, 3,000 cubic feet in bulk. It had two wings in the gallery which was suspended underneath the balloon. It rose with four persons, among others the Duke of Chartres. They were soon lost to sight in the clouds, which were very thick, and wherein they met with a violent storm. But they rose above it and met with the sun, which expanded the air of their balloon so much, as they were unable to open the valve of it, that they were obliged to tear it, and they landed about two miles from the starting point.

The somewhat idealized military costumes here, along with Indians and Quakers (foreground), were probably familiar to Robert Morton and Anne Rawle as troops moved into, out of, and around Philadelphia. From *A Pictorial Field Book of the Revolution* by B. J. Lossing, 1900.

Pert Sally Wister shows her independence even in silhouette by wearing a bow on her plain Quaker bonnet. Her journal entry here describes her first encounter with "the Major." From *Sally Wister's Journal*, edited by A. C. Myers, 1902.

At odds with Eben Denny's view of the Yorktown surrender, this engraving shows the French at left, the Americans at right, and the British in the center—all formality before British troops disappeared into town for a day of drunkenness. 1781.

Wit's Magazine, March 1783, spoofs British propaganda in this cartoon of Washington, in woman's dress, "bestowing thirteen stripes on Britania." The international implications of the Revolution are plainly seen in the other characters: a Dutchman, a Frenchman, and a Spaniard, all waiting to pick up the pieces.

Nabby Adams, in an engraving based on a J. S. Copley portrait, at about the time she wrote the diary excerpted here. From *The Republican Court* by R. W. Griswold, 1855.

Benny Bache and grandfather Ben Franklin shared their fascination with balloons, as this scene of the Montgolfier brothers' 1783 flight shows. Those experiments led to a new age of inquiry, although sometimes they produced such scientific dead-ends as hypnotizing trees.

Weatherwise's Town and Country Almanack (1782) depicted the Revolution's end. While Columbia relaxes against a liberty tree at right, Britannia weeps at the loss of trade, now enjoyed by French, Dutch, and Spanish ships. The Spirit of Evil smirks behind her while traitor Benedict Arnold hangs in New York, at right.

September 19. I went with my grandpapa to the Abbé Armons' to see the balloon of the Messrs. Roberts Brothers which was about to start. I pointed the telescope. At eleven o'clock everything was ready, and the balloon should have started. My grandpapa was playing chess, and told me to inform him as soon as I saw it start.

Three minutes before twelve I heard a cannon fired, and, a minute afterwards I saw the balloon rise. Everybody was looking. The wind was south, a little to the west. I leave the Abbé's and come with a telescope to take my place upon the roof of our house, where I found Mr. Williams. Everyone looked through the telescope in turn.

It was in the shape of a cylinder, terminated by two hemispheres. I have not been able to learn its dimensions. The aeronauts tried to drive a little against the wind by means of little oars which they had, but this did not succeed.

1785

January 14. Dr. Jeffries is come to see my grandpapa. He and Mr. Blanchard crossed the sea on the seventh of January from Dover to Calais in an aerostat.

January 15. Mr. Blanchard and his companion were to dine at our house today, but only Dr. Jeffries has come. They started from Dover with their balloon already full of holes. After having been over the sea for an hour, their balloon, still losing its gas, sank considerably. This accident compelled them to throw out all their ballast. This having again happened several times, they were compelled to throw out, first, all the ornaments of their car—namely, the painted cloth and garlands which adorned it; secondly, all their clothes except their shirts and Mr. Jeffries's cork vest, which he had provided for himself to be able to exist for some time upon the sea if he was obliged to come to that extremity (and, indeed, they had thought of throwing it out, but Mr. Blanchard opposed it), and in two hours and three-quarters they came down on the top of a tree. There they remained for twenty-eight minutes in their shirts, and from there they went to Calais where they have been carried as if in triumph.

. . .

July 12. We were to set out from Passy early yesterday, but the departure was then postponed until today. At four o'clock in the morning my grandfather's litter came, but again we were unable to start because of the number of accounts my grandfather had to settle. We positively resolved to start after dinner, and we accomplished our design at ten minutes after five in the evening. After having dined at Mr. de Chaumont's, my grandfather ascended his litter in the midst of a very great concourse of people of Passy. A mournful silence reigned around him and was only interrupted by sobs.

—"Early Notices of Ballooning
and Animal Magnetism,"
Historical Magazine 9 (1865): 209–10;
"Dr. Franklin's Return from France,"
Historical Magazine 10 (1866): 213–14.

Part VI

☆ ☆ ☆

New Americans
at Home

1786–1789

The birth of a new nation took more than merely changing words from "We the people of the states" to "We the people of the United States." Drafting the new Constitution was only the first step. It had to be ratified by each of the thirteen state conventions held for the purpose, and these became the new battlegrounds for the old conflict between state *vs.* state and region *vs.* region, this time aggravated by fear of a new form of central government that had never been tried before.

Old firebrands like Patrick Henry fought against ratifying the new Constitution as they had fought against the monarchy of Britain. New England's Elbridge Gerry even left the Constitutional Convention rather than be a party to a new Constitution that did not have a Bill of Rights to protect people from abuse by the centralized government now proposed.

Others felt just as strongly on that point. The Massachusetts convention would not ratify. Virginia's voted to ratify by a squeaky-thin majority. So did New York, despite the fact that supporters of the new Constitution, called Federalists, issued a stream of "Federalist Papers." Authored by Virginia's James Madison along with New Yorkers Alexander Hamilton and John Jay, these set out the principles of the proposed government with both argument and polemic. The spirit of compromise that had forged these principles now helped achieve ratification. If states would ratify, Madison promised, he would push a Bill of Rights through the first meeting of the new Congress—and he did.

Children born in the year that saw repeal of the Stamp Act, 1766, came of legal age the year that saw the Constitutional Convention of 1787 invent a new kind of nation. The Revolution was not complete, for the new government had yet to be formed, much less tested, but the young persons who grew up in the previous twenty years could now see themselves as something special in the eyes of the western world. Their country's defeat of the Old World's most powerful military force provided a sense of security to offset the fear of interference by a future British invasion or French subversion. Most realized for the first time a sense of community that could become national in scope.

Some, like Lucinda Lee, whose diary is excerpted here, tried to recapture the life their parents had enjoyed on their Virginia plantations, but her words reflect changes in the way Southern girls viewed themselves and their suitors. Gone were many of the trappings of chivalry that had enveloped women in an aura of gracious divinity. Even the ladies of the house were now not ashamed to do hair or sew—work that had once been done only by slaves. The new spirit of political liberty abroad in the land had percolated down to levels where gentlemen now appeared in drag to tease girls who no longer felt it necessary always to play the coquette.

College boys, too, tried to recapture the old hell-raising attitude toward school their fathers had enjoyed. Now some, like John Quincy Adams, brought a new seriousness of purpose to education, while those who had postponed their schooling until the war's end displayed a new maturity. Maturity was necessary for the decisions these young men faced not only in choosing a new kind of representative government, but in making a wise choice of life. The new nation offered seemingly boundless land and open-ended opportunity to the majority population, and a new middle class aristocracy, based on political power rather than wealth, was in the making.

Still, the heritage of British customs and precedents was tough to kill and continued to shape government in odd ways.

The Constitution gave only the oath of office for George Washington's inauguration in 1789, so the ceremony took its precedents from the coronation of George III. As Bob Lewis, the president-to-be's teenaged nephew and secretary escorted Martha Washington north to the capital, the American people still had no idea what to call the president. When Washington himself arrived in New York City it was like an emperor, with roses strewn before him, thirteen pilots to row him across the harbor, and a purple carpet rolled out for his first steps on shore. Americans didn't *become* American overnight.

In spite of the heady principles of equality that infused the land, one institution contradicted everything the new nation claimed it stood for. That was slavery. The attendees at the Constitutional Convention had recognized this, but offered no resolution. Indeed, they institutionalized inequality by declaring that only three-fifths of a state's slaves could be counted in apportioning congressman, and by allowing the importation of slaves to continue until 1808. Although Virginia had allowed owners to free their slaves at will in 1782, and in eight years the census shows 10,000 were freed there, the Northwest Ordinance of 1787, which outlawed slavery in existing western territories, said nothing about territories to open up after that. The doors were left wide open, however tacitly, on the slavery issue, and there was plenty of fertile ground for the seeds of what would become the Civil War to take root and flourish.

ON THE HOUSE PARTY CIRCUIT

Lucinda Lee, age 16?

Various plantations, Virginia, 1787

*L*ucy's journal in the form of letters provides a lively picture of teen
social life in the plantation country of Virginia. Daughter of
Thomas Ludlow Lee, "the most popular man in Virginia," according
to John Adams, she was welcome everywhere and so spent her time
riding from one house party to another, sleeping over with friends,
dancing the nights away and sometimes the days, too. Some balls
went on for four or five days without stopping, although these were
not the extravaganzas made popular today by Hollywood. Lucy's
friends danced to a single fiddler, and when he got sick, they played
games which are the ancestors of today's kissing games like "Spin the
Bottle."

She also mentions the freedoms young men took with girls,
whether the girls liked it or not. What today might be considered
sexual harassment was, for Lucy, simply unwanted attention on the

part of a friend's spirited husband. Interestingly, in spite of the drinking and partying around her, Lucy shows a predisposition for self-improvement that seems a particularly American trait. She finds pleasure with books, and prefers good sense to beauty. But like many young people before and since, Lucy is agog about clothes and is not above raiding the food cellar for a late night feast in bed.

☆   ☆   ☆

September 22. We have supped, and the gentlemen are not returned yet. Lucy and myself are in a peck of troubles for fear they should return drunk. Sister has had our bed moved into her room. Just as we were undressed and going to bed, the gentlemen arrived, and we had to scamper. Both tipsy!

October 6. Read something improving. Books of instruction will be a thousand times more pleasing after a little while than all the novels in the world. I own myself, I am too fond of novel-reading, but, by accustoming myself to reading other books, I have become less so.

October 7. I have been very busy today working a little screen to hold in my hand to prevent the fire from burning my face. I think it will be beautiful. I have seated myself in my wrapper to scribble a little. Mr. Pinkard has been reading a play all the evening to Nancy and myself. We were much pleased with it.

October 11. Hannah and myself were going to take a long walk this evening but were prevented by the two horrid mortals, Mr. Pinkard and Mr. [Corbin] Washington [Hannah's husband], who seized me and kissed me a dozen times in spite of all the resistance I could make. They really think, now they are married, they are privileged to do anything.

October 13. It is in the evening. Two beaus just come. Mrs. Pinkard tells me I must go out and let her introduce them to me. The first I am acquainted with. He is homely but a mighty worthy man. The second I never saw before. He is tolerably clever.

October 16. I don't know when I've been happier than I am now. Everything conspires to make me so. Cousin Turberville is so affectionate. She does everything in her power to make her company happy. I had forgot to tell you about Cousin Hannah's dress yesterday. It was a blue lutestring habit, taffeta apron and handkerchief, with the most beautiful little hat on the side of her head I ever saw. We are dressing for dinner. This is a ceremony always practiced here. I wear my greatcoat. We are just done tea and are having the same gentlemen to dance with again tonight.

October 17. We danced last night, and everyone appeared to be happy. I can answer for your Lucy. My partner was Mr. James Thomson, one of the best dancers I ever saw. Early this morning came one of the Misses Ballendines, truly amiable, I believe, but not handsome. But how preferable is good sense and affability to beauty, more pleasing a thousand times! The old man being sick that plays the fiddle, we have diverted ourselves playing "Grind the Bottle" and "Hide the Thimble." Our time passed away agreeably enough.

October 18. We have the addition of two more gentlemen tonight: a Doctor Harrington, a handsome man, I think, and an elderly gentleman, Captain Grigg, the most laughable creature I ever saw. They tell me I shall be highly diverted at the minuet he dances, and we intend to make him dance one tonight.

October 19. I don't think I ever laughed so much in my life as I did last night at Captain Grigg's minuet. I wish you could see him. It is really the most ludicrous thing I ever saw; and what makes it more so is, he thinks he dances a most delightful one.

October 20. Today is disagreeable and rainy. The young ladies have been showing us the wedding clothes and some dresses they had from London, very genteel and pretty. Mr. Newton is still here and is, I think, a very disagreeable creature. I wonder how Nancy did to bear with him. The young ladies have been singing for me. They are mighty obliging and sing whenever they are asked it.

October 23. We went to Mr. Thomson's, returned, and danced at night. I really have a great affection for Mrs. Pinkard. She always chooses my head-dress, dresses my hair, and is the best creature in lending you anything. If you just say you want a thing, if she happens to have it, she will insist on your wearing it. Cousin Hannah has a quantity of clothes. She has put on every day since I have been here a different dress of muslin, and all handsome.

October 27. When we got here [Bushfield plantation] we found the house pretty full. About sunset Nancy, Milly, and myself took a walk in the garden. It is a most beautiful place. We were mighty busy cutting thistles to try our sweethearts ["He loves me, he loves me not"] when Mr. Washington caught us, and you can't conceive how he plagued us—chased us all over the garden and was quite impertinent.

I must tell you of our frolic after we went in our room. We took it into our heads to want to eat. Well, we had a large dish of bacon and beef; after that, a bowl of sago cream; and after that, an apple pie. While we were eating the apple pie in bed—God bless you! making a great noise—in came Mr. Washington, dressed in Hannah's short gown and petticoat, and seized me and kissed me twenty times, in spite of all the resistance I could make, and then Cousin Molly. Hannah soon followed, dressed in his coat. They joined us in eating the apple pie and then went out. After this we took it in our heads to want to eat oysters. We got up, put on our wrappers, and went down in the cellar to get them. Do you think Mr. Washington did not follow us and scare us just to death? We went up, though, and ate our oysters. We slept in the old lady's room too, and she sat laughing fit to kill herself at us.

—Emily Mason, ed.
Journal of a Young Lady of Virginia
by Lucinda Lee Orr
(Baltimore: J. Murphy, 1871).

THE HARVARD LIFE
AND TAX REFORM

John Quincy Adams, age 19
Cambridge, Massachusetts, 1786

J. Q. Adams, brother of Nabby and future sixth president of the United States, had returned from Europe earlier than his family so that he might continue his education at Harvard. His diary tells stories about truly infantile college pranks, such as getting drunk, breaking windows, hissing the faculty, and then throwing potatoes at them. "This is certainly a proof that the spirit of liberty in the Americans of the last century has not been underrated," wrote his grandson Henry, when he published excerpts from the diary in 1872. At the same time, J. Q. also realizes the seriousness of reports from western Massachusetts about farmers resisting taxes, suffering foreclosures, and finally, attacking the federal arsenal for arms to march on the state capital in what we know today as Shay's Rebellion.

The inability of the free colonies to protect arsenals, much less regulate internal taxes, reinforced the growing sentiment for revamp-

ing the Articles of Confederation that had created a United States in name only—little more than thirteen sovereign nations rather than one nation indivisible. The subsequent convention would produce the Constitution of 1787, thus creating a "responsible national government." Still, on the threshold of these unprecedented achievements, J. Q. confesses his diary consists of "trivial events," even "a heap of trash," though Henry Adams calls the diarist's mind "almost unduly mature."

☆ ☆ ☆

March 15. The sophomore class had what is called in College a high-go. They assembled all together in the chamber of one of the class, where some of them got drunk, then sallied out and broke a number of windows for three of the tutors [teachers], and after this sublime manoeuvre staggered to their chambers. Such are the great achievements of many of the sons of Harvard! Such the delights of many of the students here!

May 31. Election Day. There is a custom among the scholars here which some of the classes follow and others do not. It is choosing a Governor and Lieutenant-Governor for the class. They commonly take some rich fellow who can treat the class now and then. The seniors this morning chose Champlin Governor and Lowell Lieutenant-Governor. The Lieutenant-Governor treated immediately, and they chose their other officers. At commons they all went into the hall in procession. Thomas, who was appointed Sheriff, marched at their head with a paper cockade in his hat and brandishing a cane in his hand instead of a sword. He conducted the Governor and Lieutenant-Governor to their seats, made his bow, and retired to the other table.

As there was a little noise in the hall, [tutor] H———

struck the handle of his knife three times on the table to still it, but instead of that almost every knife in the hall was struck on the table three times. At last the tutors rose, and as they were going out, about half a dozen fellows hissed them. They were enraged, turned round and looked as if they would devour us, but they did not discover one person, which made them look silly enough. When they turned their backs again, there was nothing but hissing and groaning and clapping hands and stamping heard in the hall, till they got into the yard, where a few potatoes were sent out to meet them. . . .

September 7. The Commonwealth is in a state of considerable fermentation. Last week at Northampton, in the County of Hampshire, a body of armed men to the number of three or four hundred prevented the Court of Common Pleas from sitting and bruised the high-sheriff dangerously, as it is reported. The same Court was likewise stopped the day before yesterday at Worcester by 400 men. The Court went to a tavern and adjourned till yesterday, and adjourned without day. The militia it seems could not be raised to quell them.

November 25. Mr. Williams gave us a lecture this forenoon, to explain astronomical instruments. Nothing new, however. There are many flying reports concerning the coming of the insurgents next week. They have been expected to arrive this evening, but none as yet have appeared. . . .

November 27. This evening, just before prayers, about 40 horsemen arrived here under the command of Judge Prescott of Groton in order to protect the court tomorrow from the rioters. We hear of nothing but Shays and Shattuck, two of the most despicable characters in the community, now [making] themselves of great consequence. There has been in the course of the day fifty different reports flying about, and not a true one among them.

December 12. The government [of the college] this morning determined that if more than half the students should be destitute of [fire] wood, the college should be dismissed.

December 13. This morning immediately after prayers, the President informed us that the vacation would begin at present and be for eight weeks and hinted that the spring vacation might on that account be omitted. As I thought I should be able to study much more conveniently here than anywhere else, I obtained leave to remain in town. Bridge proposes staying likewise, and we shall live together. Bridge engaged for us both to board at Professor Wigglesworth's.

December 18. The young ladies at Mr. Wigglesworth's dined at Judge Dana's. I went down there with Bridge to tea and passed the evening very sociably. The conversation turned upon diverse topics, and among the rest upon love, which is almost always the case when there are ladies present.

December 20. I have been rather more attentive this day than for this week past and have written considerably. This evening a sleigh came from Petersham for Baron and Whitney. The person who came with it informs us that the insurgents have all disbanded, that numbers of them suffered extremely in the late [winter] storms, one or two perished, and several still remain very ill at Worcester. They have had time to reflect on their conduct, and for their enthusiasm to cool down. I wish it may reform them.

December 31. This day completes two years since I attempted to commit to paper the transactions which daily occurred in which I was concerned. It is a question whether amidst the quantity of trivial events to which I have given place and the heap of trash which I have here inserted, there is sufficient matter worthy of writing. For these 15 months, the scenes before me have been so much alike that these pages have not even the small merit of variety. But to myself I have always spoken, for myself I have always written, and to myself only I am accountable for the nonsense and folly in this and the preceding volume.

—Henry Adams, "Harvard College, 1786–7,"
North American Review 104 (1872): 110–47;
and D. G. Allen et *al.*, eds.
The Diary of John Quincy Adams
(Cambridge, Mass.: Harvard University Press, 1981),
Vol. 1: 222, 274–75, 379–80; Vol. 2: 91–92, 145.

ESCORTING THE FIRST
"FIRST LADY"

Robert Lewis, age 19
Virginia & Maryland, 1789

A son of Washington's favorite sister, Betty, Bob Lewis served as
his uncle's secretary at age nineteen. He and one other secretary
were responsible for the paperwork during the crucial first year of the
presidency. Everything that Washington did during that year set a
precedent followed to the present day. Every official meeting and
decision had to be documented, copied, and filed for reference. That
was Bob's job.

The position required good penmanship, patience, and fortitude.
Besides keeping records and copying, Bob also had to act as his Aunt
Martha's escort during Uncle George's absence. The pay was very low
but he was given a clothing allowance and lived as part of the
Washington household. He was thus treated as one of the family even
by outsiders eager to make points with the first "first family," as Bob
learns in escorting Aunt Martha to New York.

Besides the obstacles of delayed starts, swollen rivers, mud, and broken carriages, the Washington entourage has to strike a happy medium between acting like royalty and being just plain folks. Many called his aunt, "Lady Washington," and didn't know how to address her husband—"Excellency," "Majesty" or what? There had never been a democratic first family before, so everything his aunt did also would set a precedent. The pressure was on Bob to watch his manners, too. He could never be quite sure whether those we would now call "groupies" were after him for love or for access to the president. But as a country boy headed for New York, then the nation's capital, he enjoyed making the arduous trip from Mount Vernon even if it meant getting up after only three hours' sleep.

☆ ☆ ☆

May 14. After taking an early dinner and making all the necessary arrangements, in which we were greatly retarded, it brought us to three o'clock in the evening, when we left Mount Vernon. The servants of the house and a number of the field negroes made their appearance to take leave of their mistress. Numbers of these poor wretches seemed much affected. My aunt equally so.

We traveled together as far as Alexandria and left my aunt at her request. [She] proceeded to Doctor Stuart's [stepfather of her grandchildren]. Thornton and myself put in at Mr. Bushrod Washington's and spent that night and the greater part of the next day until the evening. Then cousin [Major] George [Washington] had in this time come from Mount Vernon. Left my friend Thornton with much regret, arrived at Dr. Stuart's where all was silent melancholy and everyone anticipated the effects of parting.

May 18. The horses were hitched by five o'clock in the morning, baggage put on, and everything in readiness to decamp when, alas! the dreaded hour appeared. So pathetic and affecting a scene I never wish to be again witness to. We at length got off by which I was greatly relieved, leaving the family in tears, the children abawling, and everything in a most lamentable situation. We arrived at the ferry opposite Georgetown about nine o'clock without anything material happening. The horses were taken out and left this side as we were to get a fresh set from Colonel Van Horn to take us on the other.

We embarked in company with Doctor Stuart, his brother, Major [George] Washington, and Mr. B. Bassett and got to Georgetown with some difficulty, the river being very full and a pretty strong current which drove us down a considerable distance and alarmed my aunt not a little. Colonel Van Horn's horses were then fixed to the coach, but my aunt preferred walking up to the tavern and to let the carriage go around—which happened very luckily. The horses not being used to breast plates, which galled them, refused to take the draft at the hill and so balked. They were lashed pretty roundly for their obstinacy by which means, with their jumping and exertions, broke one of the swingle trees and the hook at the pole end of the carriage.

Colonel Van Horn then had to send in the country for other horses. Meanwhile, the repairs to the carriage was doing, which detained us two hours.

Under all these misfortunes, we again made a second attempt and succeeded, pursued our route to Bladensburg, and got there at one o'clock. Took a cold cut with some wine to stay our appetites until we should get to Major Snowden's where we proposed to quarter that night. The country about this little village is very pretty and under good cultivation. I was delighted with their meadows, orchards, etc. I likewise called on a Mr. Campbell of this place with my written instructions to endeavor to purchase a horse which my uncle had taken a fancy to, being a match for his riding horse. Mr. Campbell was from home, at Baltimore, 'twas said, where I flattered myself I should see him.

After refreshing ourselves and horses, we parted with our escorts—the gentlemen before mentioned—our company now consisting of Mrs. Washington, the children, Colonel Van Horn and self. We again set out for Major Snowden's, where we arrived at four o'clock in the evening. The roads were extremely narrow, muddy and bad—the [carriage] got hung between two trees which were scarcely wide enough to admit it. We were treated with great hospitality and civility by the major and his wife, who were very plain, honest kind of folks and made every effort to make our stay as agreeable as possible.

I found myself a good deal indisposed with a headache and, I thought, a fever, owing to a foolish young colt which I had to ride but walked, and requested that I might go to bed, which was readily granted. Happily relieved by the purchase of a horse from Mr. Campbell, who came to Major Snowden's shortly after us.

May 19. The morning was lowering and looked like rain. We were entreated to stay all day but to no effect. We had made our arrangements and it was impossible, so therefore took leave of our kind hostess who insisted that we should always make that a stage whenever we traveled that road. Major Snowden accompanied us ten or a dozen miles to show a near way and the best road. In conversation I discovered him to be a man of no inconsiderable possessions, having got a large fortune by his wife, who was an heiress to an immense estate and married him merely for love, he being a very handsome man of obscure parentage and no property. Mrs. Snowden is of the middle stature, is between 25 or 30 years of age, remarkably loquacious but sensible. She's very homely herself, but has several of the handsomest children I ever beheld. The major is nearly six feet high and proportionably bulky. His physiognomy is prepossessing but the nonsense and egotism which he is lavish in his own favor cannot [be] borne with. He's likewise talkative. The qualification seems hereditary, as it has descended from the parents to the children, who are also as vociferous and have as great volubility of tongue as parrots.

We proceeded as far as Spurrier's ordinary [bar room] and there refreshed ourselves and horses, parted with our kind conductor, previous to which I discovered him to be a complete horse jockey. Mrs. Washington shifted herself here, expecting to be met by numbers of gentlemen out of Baltimore in which time we had everything in readiness—the carriage, horses, etc. all at the door in waiting.

Our journey commenced again. The treatment I had met with the preceding night afforded me matter for contemplation at least four miles, when I was interrupted by Colonel Van Horn who had in this time been before me some distance. We had ascended an eminence and nearly reached the summit before I was disturbed in my cogitations by an exclamation or shout from the colonel desiring me to observe the most beautiful prospect I had ever seen. Fond of seeing anything remarkable or curious, I quickened my pace and soon came up with him when to my utmost astonishment, after having traveled through a barren uncultivated soil, I beheld one of the most beautiful and yet limited landscapes I had ever seen in my life. The bottom of this hill is washed by the Patuxent River which forms an angle or elbow. In the extension corner is situated a little village called Elk Ridge, which is irregular but the houses small and neat and yet well built. This river takes its source near Frederick Town and runs a pretty direct course until it comes to this place, from whence it meanders in an east direction until it disembogues itself into the Chesapeake. The farms which are situated on each side of this river are under the highest cultivation, interspersed with orchards, meadows, etc. which form the most beautiful landscape that can be imagined. This prospect is bounded all round with large hills or mountains which intercept a more extensive view.

We coasted along down this river through the plantations before mentioned. You are admitted into these places by large gates which are kept up at the expense of the state of Maryland and are very common throughout the whole state. We arrived at the ferry, which is not more than 40 yards wide but very deep. We observed a number of small craft going up to Elk River. There being a stiff breeze and the tide in their favor we supposed them to run at the rate of ten knots an hour.

We put the coach on board the boat, leaving the horses and servants behind, and embarked. The wind by this time had risen almost to a storm. The waves running very high, the boat took in a great deal of water, which frightened my aunt a good deal. However, by the exertions of our ferryman with the assistance of Colonel Van Horn and myself, we reached the opposite shore where we were met by several gentlemen from Baltimore who had come out for the purpose of escorting Mrs. Washington into town.

Mrs. Carrol, expecting Mrs. Washington, had made considerable preparation. We found a large bowl of salubrious ice punch, with fruits, etc. which had been plucked from the trees in a greenhouse, lying on the tables in great abundance.

These, after riding 25 or 30 mile without eating or drinking, was no unwelcome luxury. However, Mrs. Carrol could not complain that we had not done her punch honor, for in the course of one quarter of an hour, the time we tarried, this bowl which held upwards of two gallons was entirely consumed, to the no little satisfaction of us all.

Colonel Ballard proposed to walk with me and show the town. In the first place, I recollected that Mr. Lyanor lived here and immediately made inquiry whereabouts—as we had once been very intimate, I was glad of an opportunity to show that I had not lost sight of our former acquaintance. He received me in a very friendly and cordial manner and as usual made the natural interrogations with respect to the people of Fredericksburg [Virginia—Bob's home]. I spent an half-hour with him, then accompanied by Colonel Ballard, returned to the doctor, where a number of ladies had assembled to pay their respects to Mrs. Washington, the names of which are too numerous to insert. Let it suffice that they were the handsomest assortment of women that I had ever seen.

I attached myself entirely to a Miss Spear, who was remarkably talkative and seemed to be pretty well acquainted with my friend Robert Mercer, which afforded considerable fund of conversation. The evening concluded with an elegant entertainment and fireworks. The company did not retire until after 11 o'clock. I saw Miss Spear home, who appeared to be much pleased with my attentions, and insisted that I would never go through Baltimore without calling on her. She entreated me to come in, but it being late, and a young gentleman in company with me, I thought it prudent to return with him, otherwise I might have lost myself. Miss Spear was extremely pressing, but as I felt better disposed for sleep than any other kind of amusement so made my bow and departed, not without first promising that, if it rained the next day, which looked a good deal like it, I would spend the day with her.

I then made haste back to the doctor's, expecting to be locked out, but was mistaken, for I found the doctor seated at table with some of the gentlemen drinking wine. I was requested to take a chair and join them but excused myself by saying it was late and that I should have to rise early in the morning, so begged that I might be indulged to go to bed. This broke up the company and I was conducted to a room neatly furnished.

May 20. Sleep was foreign from eyes. The hurry and bustle that I had been in all day, and the variety which I had seen, gave sufficient scope to my imagination. To sleep was impossible. These agreeable reflections was interrupted, for we were serenaded [by the townspeople] until two o'clock in the morning, when I fell asleep—and was waked by the clock striking five, which was the hour we proposed leaving town to avoid any parade that might be intended.

. .

New York

July 4. This being the thirteenth year since the Declaration of Independence and the commencement of a new era, every heart seems to expand with joy and every face bears the marks of pleasure and satisfaction.

The morn was ushered in with a salute of 13 cannon

from the Battery, the ringing of bells, and every other demonstration of joy which a happy and independent people alone can experience.

—Manuscript,
Mount Vernon Ladies' Association Library,
Mount Vernon, Virginia.

AFTERWORD

Abigail Adams (Jr.) wed while in London. She married an ex-aide to George Washington, William Smith, who hoped to profit from his new family connection but was too feather-headed to hold a job long. He was constantly gambling and venturing into wild schemes, like liberating Venezuela, while poor Nabby lived isolated in a cabin on New York State's wild frontier with three small children. Independent to the end, she refused her family's offer of help until, suffering from breast cancer, she returned to die in 1813 at her brother John Quincy Adams's home.

John Quincy Adams went on to a brilliant career in the diplomatic service as minister to Russia, then Secretary of State, and then our sixth president. Afterwards he returned to serve as a long-term congressman, playing a vitally active role in trying to abolish slavery or at least keep it out of the new territories. His mother always treated him like a boy. When he was first in Congress, she urged her daughter-in-law to make sure that John always had a good breakfast and carried a cracker in his pocket. He died in 1848.

Betsy Ambler, by marrying into the Brent family, became connected to the Carrolls who owned large portions of Maryland, but her husband William died in the war. She then wed Edward Carrington, a high-ranking officer and close friend of George Washington, with whom they often visited. General

191

Carrington's death left her again a wealthy widow, this time until her death in 1810 thirty years later.

Benjamin Franklin Bache, having been taught printing by his grandfather in France, returned to America to publish a newspaper known as *The Aurora* which, in its violent opposition, very likely made Washington so mad he would not run for a third term as president. President John Adams had Benny thrown in jail under the Alien and Sedition Act, but Benny outwitted further prosecution. Succumbing to yellow fever in 1798 at age 29, he nevertheless had prepared his widow to carry on the newspaper's unremitting attacks against the Federalists and in favor of Thomas Jefferson's presidency.

Elijah Backus returned from the war to take a political job as port officer in New London, Connecticut, while studying law. Passing the bar, he joined his brothers in migrating to the new town of Marietta, Ohio, where Elijah founded *The Gazette* which he edited and used as a springboard into local politics until his death a dozen years later in 1811.

Oliver Boardman's family had pioneered Connecticut settlement at Wethersfield and his father had a thriving cabinetmaking and shipbuilding trade in Middletown, but Oliver and wife Sarah Danforth settled down in Hartford to raise their seven boys and four girls until, in Oliver's forty-fourth year, their youngest was born. Thereafter the record is silent.

Charles Bourgatte, sometimes called Charlotte, had been an indentured servant of Edward Manwaring up in the Gaspé peninsula. Because of his testimony at the Boston Massacre trials, Manwaring and another customs officer named Monroe, along with two others, were sent to jail for a week. When Charles was convicted of perjury, he escaped jail but had to stand in the pillory an hour, take twenty-five lashes on his bare back, and somehow pay the court costs for his trial. How he paid is as mysterious as what happened to him ever after.

Jemima Condict did listen to her heart instead of other people's gossip. She married her cousin, Aaron Harrison. Their marriage was all too brief, for she died at age 24 giving birth to their only child, Ira, in 1779.

Ebenezer Denny remained in the army after the war, pacifying tribes in the Northwest Territory until retiring in 1792. He settled in Pittsburgh as its first mayor, enjoying health, wealth and honor until his death in 1822.

Solomon Drowne spent the war as ship's surgeon, a noble sacrifice since he was subject to seasickness. After the war he wandered across Europe and then, by sheer coincidence, also settled in Marietta, Ohio, where Elijah Backus lived. Restless, Drowne moved his five daughters and three sons to Virginia before finally returning to Rhode Island where Brown University gave him a medical degree and named him Professor of Botany. He died in 1834.

Rebecca Franks remained on Long Island while the war lasted and then went to England with the British army. She wed a colonel, Sir Henry Johnson, and had two sons. Both joined the British army. The younger was killed in the War of 1812. She died in the fashionable resort town of Bath, England in 1823.

Charles Herbert, freed from prison in a prisoner exchange, returned to his native Newburyport, Massachusetts in 1780, married Molly Butler, developed a successful business as a cabinetmaker, and died in September 1808 leaving fourteen living children.

Baylor Hill was also freed in a prisoner exchange so that he was able to be present at the surrender of Cornwallis at Yorktown. His meritorious service earned him a soldier's bounty of land instead of dollars. He was thus able to parlay 5,666 acres of land in the western territories into a successful career in finance. He wed Mary Brooke, served as mayor of Norfolk, Virginia, and lived until at least 1839.

Martha Jefferson married her cousin Thomas Mann Randolph within months after returning from Paris. He, too, had been educated in Europe but had probably not romanced her there: Their marriage seems to have been an impulsive affair. They had a dozen children, the youngest celebrated as the first born in the White House. Widowed in 1828 with four boys and four girls to raise, she was about to open a school when state legislatures gave her a pension out of respect for her father, who had died bankrupt. She died from a stroke at age 64.

Lucinda Lee left her native plantation, Bellevue, to wed Dr. John Dalrymple Orr. They had two daughters who married equally well, with Ellen (Mrs. Asa Rogers) becoming a celebrated belle of the Washington, D.C. social scene. Lucy's vital statistics did not survive the Civil War.

Robert Lewis had to leave his job in New York City when he wished to marry his girl back home, Judith Browne. President Washington had a policy dating back to military days of not employing married men on his staff. Bob returned to Virginia where he acted as Washington's real estate agent, collecting rents and the like, on his uncle's extensive land holdings. He sometimes also served as mayor of his native Fredericksburg until his death in 1829, at age 60.

Robert Morton survived the British occupation and wed his half-sister Hannah before the war ended, but he could not escape the customary fevers that ravaged Philadelphia summers and so died in 1786, age 26. Hannah died two years later of the same fever, and so both predeceased their parents.

Anne Rawle married wealthy Philadelphia merchant John Clifford. They had three girls and a boy, but only one girl survived childhood. Anne's mother and stepfather, exiled during the war, returned to live with her in Burlington, New Jersey until they could obtain legal restitution of what they had lost in war. Anne died in 1828.

Nancy Shippen never did reconcile with her mean husband, nor would she give him a divorce for fear he would take custody of their child. Baby Peggy lived with Grandma Livingston until age 16, when she elected to live with Nancy in Philadelphia. Peggy never married. She and Nancy lived like Protestant nuns, prey to every conman purporting to promote religion. Nancy died at 78, Peggy at 82.

Slave Andrew, as a slave, left no life records at all even though his master, reputable merchant (and Son of Liberty) Oliver Wendell testified that he could read and, more rare for a slave, write. Prosecutor Robert Treat Paine also accused him of being a poet in hopes thereby of tainting his testimony. Today Andrew's notoriety stems from having testified that Crispus Attucks was the attacker rather than the victim at the Boston Massacre, thus tending to subvert Attucks's standing as a hero.

Samuel Webb, after nine years in the army, settled in New York to seek his fortune as a merchant and in politics. The best he could do in politics was to serve as one of the masters of ceremony for Washington's inauguration, but he was very active in the Order of the Cincinnati, an elitist organization of veteran officers somewhat like today's American Legion. He finally wed Catherine Hogeboom and moved to rural Claverack, New York, to become a gentleman farmer till his death in 1807.

Anna Winslow died from tuberculosis in Marshfield, Massachusetts, then a center for loyalists to King George III. Her death could not be recorded officially in Boston, but we know that she died in 1779 at age 20.

Sally Wister never married but spent her life nursing her invalid mother, dying just a couple of months after her mother died in 1804. Her major also died young, from a war-related ailment. His real name was William Truman Stoddert.